UNDERSTANDING
INTRUSION DETECTION
THROUGH VISUALIZATION

Advances in Information Security

Sushil Jajodia

Consulting Editor
Center for Secure Information Systems
George Mason University
Fairfax, VA 22030-4444
email: jajodia@gmu.edu

The goals of the Springer International Series on ADVANCES IN INFORMATION SECURITY are, one, to establish the state of the art of, and set the course for future research in information security and, two, to serve as a central reference source for advanced and timely topics in information security research and development. The scope of this series includes all aspects of computer and network security and related areas such as fault tolerance and software assurance.

ADVANCES IN INFORMATION SECURITY aims to publish thorough and cohesive overviews of specific topics in information security, as well as works that are larger in scope or that contain more detailed background information than can be accommodated in shorter survey articles. The series also serves as a forum for topics that may not have reached a level of maturity to warrant a comprehensive textbook treatment.

Researchers, as well as developers, are encouraged to contact Professor Sushil Jajodia with ideas for books under this series.

Additional titles in the series:

HOP INTEGRITY IN THE INTERNET by Chin-Tser Huang and Mohamed G. Gouda; ISBN-10: 0-387-24426-3

PRIVACY PRESERVING DATA MINING by Jaideep Vaidya, Chris Clifton and Michael Zhu; ISBN-10: 0-387- 25886-8

BIOMETRIC USER AUTHENTICATION FOR IT SECURITY: From Fundamentals to Handwriting by Claus Vielhauer; ISBN-10: 0-387-26194-X

IMPACTS AND RISK ASSESSMENT OF TECHNOLOGY FOR INTERNET SECURITY:Enabled Information Small-Medium Enterprises (TEISMES) by Charles A. Shoniregun; ISBN-10: 0-387-24343-7

SECURITY IN E-LEARNING by Edgar R. Weippl; ISBN: 0-387-24341-0

IMAGE AND VIDEO ENCRYPTION: From Digital Rights Management to Secured Personal Communication by Andreas Uhl and Andreas Pommer; ISBN: 0-387-23402-0

INTRUSION DETECTION AND CORRELATION: Challenges and Solutions by Christopher Kruegel, Fredrik Valeur and Giovanni Vigna; ISBN: 0-387-23398-9

THE AUSTIN PROTOCOL COMPILER by Tommy M. McGuire and Mohamed G. Gouda; ISBN: 0-387-23227-3

ECONOMICS OF INFORMATION SECURITY by L. Jean Camp and Stephen Lewis; ISBN: 1-4020-8089-1

PRIMALITY TESTING AND INTEGER FACTORIZATION IN PUBLIC KEY CRYPTOGRAPHY by Song Y. Yan; ISBN: 1-4020-7649-5

SYNCHRONIZING E-SECURITY by Godfried B. Williams; ISBN: 1-4020-7646-0

Additional information about this series can be obtained from http://www.springeronline.com

UNDERSTANDING INTRUSION DETECTION THROUGH VISUALIZATION

by

Stefan Axelsson
Chalmers University of Technology
Göteborg, Sweden

David Sands
Chalmers University of Technology
Göteborg, Sweden

 Springer

Dr. Stefan Axelsson
Dept. of Computer Science and Engineering
Chalmers University of Technology
412 96 GÖTEBORG
SWEDEN

Prof. David Sands
Dept. of Computer Science and Engineering
Chalmers University of Technology
412 96 GÖTEBORG
SWEDEN

Library of Congress Control Number: 2005933712

UNDERSTANDING INTRUSION DETECTION THROUGH VISUALIZATION
by Stefan Axelsson and David Sands

ISBN-13: 978-0-387-27634-2
ISBN-10: 0-387-27634-3
e-ISBN-13: 978-0-387-27636-6
e-ISBN-10: 0-387-27636-X

Printed on acid-free paper.

Printed in the United States of America.

9 8 7 6 5 4 3 2 1   SPIN 11425250, 11524885

springeronline.com

Contents

List of Figures

List of Tables

Foreword

This monograph is the outgrowth of Stefan Axelson's PhD Dissertation at Chalmers University in Göteborg, Sweden. The dissertation, in turn collects a number of research efforts performed over a period of six years or so into a coherent whole. It was my honor to serve as the "opponent" at Dr. Axelsson's examination. In the Swedish system, it is the job of the opponent to place the candidate's work into a broader perspective, demonstrating its significance and contributions to the field and then to introduce the work to the attendees at the examination. This done, the candidate presents the technical details of the work and the opponent critiques the work giving the candidate the opportunity to defend it[1]. This forward is adapted from the introduction that I gave at the examination and should serve to acquaint the reader, not only with the work at hand, but also with the field to which it applies. The title of the work, "Understanding Intrusion Detection Through Visualization," is particularly telling. As is the case with any good piece of research, we hope to gain an understanding of a problem, not just a recipe or simple solution of immediate, but limited utility.

For much of its formative period, computer security concentrated on developing systems that, in effect, embodied a fortress model of protection. These systems were intended to be immune to most of the attacks that we see today and were supposed to be capable of processing classified material at multiple levels of security (MLS). The problem of building highly secure systems was harder than thought, but, by the early 1990s, a number of promising systems were beginning to emerge.

In the mid 1980s commodity personal computers emerged. These were initially produced without any regard for security – not even protecting the user

---

[1] It is interesting to note that Swedish technical universities received the ability to award PhDs rather late (1940 in the case of Chalmers), as it was felt that the work of the master engineer had to stand above *any* criticism and it was thus inappropriate to subject it to a form of examination which in its very form relied on the work being subjected to critique.

from himself. The military adopted these platforms wholesale in spite of their insecurity and stopped substantial MLS research efforts in the mid 1990s.

By the late 1980s, broad band networks were available to most corporations and to many educational institutions. Increasingly, these were using PC based platforms as network nodes. Node level security was minimal and difficult. Managing large numbers of machines securely was difficult or impossible. Firewalls were introduced to provide a single point of protection for an organization. Intrusion Detection Systems (IDS) were introduced to detect attacks either from the outside or from the inside, providing another line of defense for the increasingly difficult to manage firewalls.

In 1980, James Anderson produced a report entitled "Computer Security Threat Monitoring and Surveillance" that sets up the framework for what we now know as intrusion detection. Anderson (and later Denning) assumed that user behavior was regular enough to permit statistical models that would equate unusual (or anomalous) with malicious. In general, this is not true, but anomaly based systems are still the focus of much research. The other primary area of activity is signature based systems in which patterns of activity that match previously known intrusions are sought. Finding the right pattern at an appropriate level of abstraction is not easy and most truly new attacks are undetectable using signatures.

There are a number of problems that beset both production and research intrusion detection systems. These provide a context for the monograph and include: 1) Lack of a fundamental theoretical basis for intrusion detection and 2) Poor understanding of environments in which intrusion detection systems function. These lead to excessive false alarms, inappropriate training for machine learning systems, poorly formed signatures for abuse detection and many other problems. The monograph directly addresses several of these problems. It is the result of a series of investigations that began late in the last century. Although individual results have appeared in a variety of forums, they represent a coherent body of work and a significant contribution to the field.

In the next few paragraphs, we will introduce each of these works and place them in perspective. The technical details of each form a chapter in the monograph.

The Base-Rate Fallacy and the Difficulty of Intrusion Detection

Originally presented at RAID 99, this was my first introduction to the Dr. Axelsson and his work. It deals with the problem of excessive false alarm rates, a problem that plagues many intrusion detection systems.

The problem of false alarms is troubling. Every alarm requires investigation and uses (typically human) resources. Alarms are often described in terms of percentages of cases examined. If there are a lot of cases, even a low alarm rate can require excessive resources to examine every alarm. While this is well known in epidemiology (where it is called the Base-Rate Fallacy), its impact was not understood in the IDS community. As a result of this work, the IDS community is now aware that very low intrusion rates require even lower false alarm rates to prevent operator overload. The consequences of this observation inform much of the subsequent work.

Visualizing Intrusions

Watching the Webserver represents a *tour de force* in primary data analysis as well as providing a beautiful example of an observational study. In many cases, the quantity of data available defies individual analyses. Only by clustering and abstraction can the data be reduced to manageable size.

Most researchers in this area are more interested in their algorithms than in the data. In this work the analysis is properly viewed as a means to understanding the processes that produced the data. While the way the log reduction and visualization were performed are significant contributions, some of the observations in the discussion have the potential to be even more significant as they provide a possible basis for defining a necessary property of certain intrusions.

Combining a Bayesian Classifier with Visualization

Understanding the IDS is an often overlooked aspect of research in this field. Much of the current work in intrusion detection involves machine learning. Even using carefully labeled data, classifiers often learn the right thing for the wrong reasons. As far as I know, the approach here of using visualization with interactive classification during the learning phase as an aid to understanding both the data and the detector, is unique.

While the simple Bayesian detector used in the study is not particularly strong as an IDS, the training approach can be extended to other detectors and the results are impressive for the detector involved. This work is significant in its own right, however, it also sets forth a significant agenda of future work.

Visualizing the Inner Workings of a Self Learning Classifier

Following the previous work with a more complex learning system is logical next step. The detector used in this study is much more complex and its operation, as originally defined, opaque. Not knowing why a classifier made a particular classification impedes training and hampers use.

The work performed here demonstrates, for this more complex case, that it is possible to develop a visualization that gives insight into both the classifier and the data allowing the "why" to be understood. As in the previous case, the insights into the reasons why the detectors function as they do on the data provides insight into the intrusive behavior.

Visualization for Intrusion Detection

Hooking the Worm is an interesting study of attempts to attack a small web server. This work takes a neutral view of the dataset involved, developing visual techniques for clustering and displaying web accesses. As we noted earlier, clustering and abstracting allow us to reduce many individual records to a manageable set of classes.

In this case, reducing the records to a few essential characteristics still allow the production of useful patterns. The primary contribution of the work is a simple mechanism for providing insight into system activity in a way that supports classification into malicious and benign activity.

Beyond the Monograph

In addition to providing specific insights in a number of specific areas of intrusion detection, a number of less tangible contributions are made. All of the studies serve as exemplars of the utility of observational studies in computer security. The astute reader will see that the work has benefited from deep thought into the activities manifest in the data and tools studied. The resulting insights are carefully and clearly set forth.

The works also show that there is no easy substitute for primary data collection and analysis. Researchers who expect to have data sets handed to them, should take note that significant results require hard and tedious work. In many other fields, primary data collection and data management may consume as much as 90% of a project's budget. There is no reason to expect observational studies in computer security to be different.

In summary, this is work to be emulated by researchers as well as students. It has been a great pleasure to correspond with Stefan Axelsson as he performed the studies leading to the thesis this monograph is based on, and it is a pleasure to be able to introduce the work to the readers of this monograph.

John McHugh
Canada Research Chair
Director, Privacy and Security Laboratory
Dalhousie University
Halifax, Nova Scotia, Canada
July 2005

Preface

With the ever increasing use of computers for critical systems, computer security, the protection of data and computer systems from intentional, malicious intervention, is attracting much attention. Among the methods for defense, *intrusion detection*, i.e. the application of a tool to help the operator identify ongoing or already perpetrated attacks, has been the subject of considerable research in the past ten years. A key problem with current intrusion detection systems is the high number of false alarms they produce. This book presents research into why false alarms are and will remain a problem, and proposes to apply results from the field of *information visualization* to the problem of intrusion detection. This approach promises to enable the operator to correctly identify false (and true) alarms, and also aid the operator in identifying other operational characteristics of intrusion detection systems. Four different visualization approaches are presented, mainly applied to data from web server access logs. The four approaches studied can be divided into *direct* and *indirect* methods. In the direct approaches the system puts the onus of identifying the malicious access requests on the operator by way of the visualization. For the indirect approaches the state of two self learning automated intrusion detection systems are visualized to enable the operator to examine their inner workings. The aim here being to provide the operator with an understanding of how the intrusion detections systems operate and whether that level of operation, and the quality of the output, is satisfactory. Several experiments were performed and many different attacks in web access data from publicly available web servers were found. The visualization helped the operator either detect the attacks herself and more importantly the false alarms.

Website

A website for the book can be found at "www.cs.chalmers.se/~dave/VisBook". Most importantly the website contains the more detailed figures from the book, in full size and color.

Acknowledgments

This book is based on the PhD thesis of the first author, under the supervision of the second. Even though writing the thesis on which this book was based was at times a lonely task, the research was not done in isolation. Far from it; I owe many more people my thanks than I can mention here. That said I would still like to take the opportunity to mention a few people who have been instrumental in helping to bring this work to completion.

While all my colleagues are too numerous to mention, I would especially like to thank (in no particular order) Daniel Hedin, Ulf Norell, Nils Anders Danielsson, Tobias Gedell, Claes Nyberg and Thorbjörn Axelsson. I would be less knowledgeable without having worked with you and I would certainly have had a much drearier time doing it. My erstwhile climbing partner, now turned colleague Dr. Rogardt Heldal deserves special mention, as he is put up with my comings and goings and still managed to provide valuable insights over the past few years. My erstwhile supervisor Prof. Erland Jonsson also deserves special mention, as he was the one that put me on to the idea of applying visualisation to the area of intrusion detection in the first place, many years ago now. I would also like to thank previous and present colleagues at the department of Computer Engineering here at Chalmers and at Ericsson where I have been employed for the past few years.

Outside of Chalmers we would like to thank Prof. John McHugh for his helpful comments and support on a number of aspects of the work presented here, and to *Spotfire inc* for letting us use "Spotfire Decision Suite" for some of our visualization experiments.

Last but not least are the two people without whose support this work would not have got far. I am talking of course of my wife Hanna Tornevall who has had to bear the brunt of the work keeping the family going this autumn, and our son Oskar. In fact, Oskar's first proper two syllable word was "dat-oo" (clearly legible Swedish for *dator*, i.e. *computer*), as in: "Oskar, where's daddy?", "Dat-oo!" I know I have been an absent father at times when preparing the thesis this book was based on, even when present in the flesh. Thank you Oskar for not holding that against me.

Stefan Axelsson

Since Stefan did all the hard work, there are considerably fewer acknowledgements needed from my side. However, this work would not have been possible without the support of the Department of Computer Science and Engineering at Chalmers, and research grants from *SSF* (the Swedish foundation for Strategic Research) and *Vinnova* (The Swedish Agency for Innovation Systems).

David Sands

Göteborg, August 2005

Chapter 1

INTRODUCTION

All science is either physics or stamp collecting.
—— Ernest Rutherford (1871–1937)

1. Context

In the early days of electronic computing, computer security was primarily of interest in military circles. With the emergence of the Internet as a household concept, computer security has become a universal concern. The general public has grown accustomed to hearing about the exploits of hackers and credit card fraudsters on the evening news, and many have first-hand experience of *phishers*, *viruses*, *worms* and the like. And as our dependence on computer infrastructure increases, so do the financial and political incentives to exploit security vulnerabilities. The computer crimes of yesterday, most of which were little more than pranks, have come of age with the realization that there are huge sums up for grabs for the enterprising criminal with a technological knack.

To counter these threats, engineering practices improve to become more security aware, and security research develops new methods for the construction of secure systems. So we might hope to reduce security flaws and vulnerabilities. But at the same time our systems are becoming ever more complex, so it is clear that security vulnerabilities are here to stay. Thus our security defenses must include mechanisms for dealing with and learning from security failures.

This book presents research into one principle of protecting valuable computer resources: *surveillance*, using *information visualization* to aid the operator in understanding the security state of the monitored system, either directly or indirectly, by providing insight into the operation of some intrusion detection system.

We continue this introductory chapter with a brief look at what we mean by *computer security*, saving a more complete overview of intrusion prevention and detection to Chapter 2.

We then present our rationale for applying the principle of information visualization to intrusion detection, together with a short introduction to visualization.

2.   Computer Security

The computer security field is primarily concerned with protecting one particular resource: data.

The value of data can be compromised in three ways, commonly referred to as the *CIA* of computer security [CEC91].

1 *Confidentiality* Prevention of the unauthorized disclosure of information.

   The value of much data relies on it being kept secret from prying eyes. Violating this secrecy thus entails a breach of confidentiality.

2 *Integrity* Prevention of the unauthorized modification of information.

   In some circumstances we may not be particular about the secrecy of our data, but it remains absolutely crucial that the data not be tampered with. We require a high level of trust in the accuracy of our data, i.e. for its integrity to remain unquestioned.

3 *Availability* Prevention of the unauthorized withholding of information or resources.

   Our data should be available to us when, where and in the form we need it. Data that is confidential and has the highest integrity will be of no use to us if we cannot process it when the need arises. Thus it is imperative that our data remains available to us at our convenience.

   An increasingly relevant fourth factor is sometimes added [Mea93, Jon98]:

4 *No unauthorized use*, viz. that no unauthorized person should be allowed to use the computing resource, even though such use in itself might not violate any of the *CIA* requirements.

From a risk management perspective, it is easy see that such a person would probably end up in a position from which further violations were possible – including the use of our computing resources to violate the *CIA* requirements of other systems, for example through participation in a distributed denial of service attack.

Different owners of data make different decisions about the relative importance of these factors. Three hypothetical scenarios will suffice as examples. The first is that of a military entity, paranoid about confidentiality to the point that it would rather blow up its own computer installations then let them fall intact into the hands of the enemy. Integrity and availability play less of a role in such a decision. The second is that of a bank. Although it is anxious that information might leak into the wrong hands, it is more concerned with integrity. That someone can learn the balance of an account is less of a concern than the risk that someone could alter it, perhaps by adding a zero to the end. The third is a relatively new and is that of an internet merchant who is mostly concerned with the continued availability of her website as while she can tolerate the odd leaked credit card number of one of her customers, she cannot tolerate having her business shut down for any appreciable amount of time. The latter scenario has become increasingly important in the last few years.

Many security measures can be employed to defend against computer intrusions and other unauthorized tampering with protected resources, the establishment of a strong perimeter defense being only one possible measure. Another method well established in the traditional security field is that of an intrusion alarm coupled with a security response. A great deal of research has recently gone into the idea of automated intrusion alarm for computer systems, a so-called *intrusion detection system*, or *IDS* for short. We postpone a detailed overview of intrusion detection until Chapter 2.

3. Rationale and Problem Statement

A significant problem with intrusion detection systems – one which we focus on in Chapter 3 – is the high number of false alarms. –It has long been known in security circles that ordinary electronic alarm systems should be circumvented during the normal operation of the facility, when supervisory staff are more likely to be lax because they are accustomed to false alarms [Pie48]. By analogy, burglar alarms operate under a very restricted security policy: any activity whatsoever on the premises is suspicious. Intrusion detection systems on the other hand are active when the computer system is in full operation, when most activity is benign. In the shop lifting scenario however, an ordinary burglar alarm would not be appropriate since there would be a multitude of normal, benign activity (the shopkeeper even encouraging this). The shoplifting problem is currently addressed among other things by *surveillance*, i.e. human supervision of the potential shoplifters. The human, using her senses unaided, is too expensive to employ directly, and therefore technology is brought to bear in the form of video cameras, video recorders, etc.

Taking the analogy with surveillance more literally leads us to the central idea of this book: the use of some form of *information visualization* to the intrusion detection problem. The work presented in this volume explores the use of simple techniques from the visualization field as means to aide the surveillance of computer systems.

Our methods are not aimed at the naive user however. The operator of any intrusion detection system *must* have a rudimentary understanding of the assets that need protection and common ways of attacking said assets. To assume otherwise would be akin to airport security staff knowing nothing the dangers of different types of firearms and sharp implements, and being oblivious to the most common methods of evading detection. A metal detector, however sophisticated, would not be of much use in such a situation, as the operator would not be able to evaluate the output. That is not to say that the staff necessarily would need to know how to *build* a metal detector. We aim for the same level of sophistication of the users of our tools.

Thus the *main* point of the investigation outlined in this book is as follows: given that false alarms are a problem with current approaches to intrusion detection: in what ways can information visualization be utilized to aid the operator in identifying false alarms?

4.   Information Visualization

We briefly mention some of the basic concepts in the field of information visualization. The visualization techniques employed in this work are all fairly simple, and build on well-known ideas. Good introductions to this area are [Spe01] and [CMS99]. This section borrows heavily from the latter.

The human mind's cognitive skills are limited. By cognition we mean "The acquisition or use of knowledge" [CMS99, p. 6]. To overcome the shortcomings of our limited cognitive skills, humans have invented external aids that help us in cognitive tasks. These aids are often in graphical form (c.f. doing longhand arithmetic using pencil and paper, where we aid limited short term memory by keeping intermediate results as glyphs on paper). The use of the external world in the aid in cognitive tasks is sometimes called "external cognition" [CMS99, p. 1]. The use of external aid is central to the effective utilization of the limited cognitive skills of the human:

> ... visual artifacts aid though; in fact, they are completely entwined with cognitive action. The progress of civilization can be read in the invention of visual artifacts, from writing to mathematics, to maps to printing to diagrams, to visual computing. As Norman says, "The real powers come from devising external aids that enhance cognitive abilities." Information visualization is about just that—exploiting the dynamic, interactive, inexpensive medium of graphical computers to device new external aids enhancing cognitive abilities. It seems obvious that it can be done. It is clear that the visual artifacts ... have profound effects on peoples' abilities to assimilate information, to compute with it, to understand it, to create new knowledge. Visual artifacts and computers do for the minds what cars do for the feet or steam shovels do for the hands. But it remains to puzzle out through cycles of system building and analysis how to build net next generation of such artifacts. (Card et. al. [CMS99, pp. 5–6]).

Information visualization then is the use of computers to give abstract data an interactive visual form. By *abstract* we mean that the data is non-physical in origin. One such origin of data that we deal with exclusively in this is log data from computer systems, especially access log data from webservers.

The information visualization process can be divided into three distinct steps:

Data transformations map *Raw Data*, that is data in some idiosyncratic format into *Data Tables*, relational descriptions of data extended to include metadata.

Visual mappings transform *Data Tables* into *Visual Structures*, structures that combine spatial substrates, marks, and graphical properties. Finally,

View transformations create *Views* of the Visual Structure by specifying graphical parameters such as position, scaling, and clipping.

User interaction controls parameters of these transformations, restricting the view to certain data ranges, for example, or changing the nature of the transformation. The visualizations and their controls are used in the service of some task. (Card et. al. [CMS99, p. 17]).

As a research area, information visualization is now some twenty years old (even though the visual presentation of data of course is much older) with rapid development in the last ten years or so due to the advent of cheap personal computers with substantial processing and graphics capabilities. This thesis follows one trend in the visualization area, away from pure information visualization studies with its goals of developing new generally applicable visualization strategies, towards application of the principles developed in the past to new problem domains.

5. Overview of the book

The theme for this book can be viewed as *false alarm suppression*, i.e. how do we make the system as a whole (including the operator) able to handle false alarms? After a brief introduction to the topic of intrusion detection in Chapter 2, the third chapter provides a key piece of motivation for the main topic of this book: it shows why false alarms are, and will always be, a problem, by explaining the issue of false alarms using the *base-rate fallacy*. The following chapters investigate the application of information visualization to the intrusion detection problem and how this helps the operator more easily identify false alarms (and detect true alarms). First the visualization of the output of an anomaly detection system—applied to unique web access request strings—is studied in Chapter 4. This study is successful but has drawbacks which are addressed in the following two chapters (Chapter 5 and Chapter 6) which develop successively more complex directed self learning detectors with integrated visualization to enable the operator to detect false (and true) alarms but also to see a visual representation of the training process, and interactively alter it. The last chapter (Chapter 7) then picks up where the previous left off by presenting a method for correlation of malicious web access request strings once they have been detected (by the previous methods for example) so that the operator may identify the entities making the requests.

We conclude this introduction with a more detailed overview of the Chapters.

Chapter 2: An Introduction to Intrusion Detection

The reader unfamiliar with the area of computer security and intrusion detection in particular will find an introduction to the area. The Chapter covers some basic terminology and concepts in the area of intrusion prevention and detection, and presents the typical architecture of an intrusion detection system.

Chapter 3: The Base-Rate Fallacy and the Difficulty of Intrusion Detection

Many different demands can be made of an intrusion detection system. An important requirement is that it be *effective*, in other words that it should detect a substantial percentage of intrusions into the supervised system while still keeping the *false alarm* rate at an acceptable level.

This chapter demonstrates that intrusion detection in a realistic setting is perhaps harder than previously thought. This is due to the base-rate fallacy problem, because of which the factor limiting the performance of an intrusion detection system is not the ability to identify intrusive behaviour correctly, but rather *its ability to suppress false alarms*. A very high standard, less than $1/100000$ false alarms per 'event' given the stated set of circumstances, has to be reached for the intrusion detection system to live up to these expectations as far as *effectiveness* is concerned. The cited studies of intrusion detector performance that were plotted and compared indicate that anomaly-based methods may have a long way to go before they can reach these standards because their false alarm rates are several orders of magnitude larger than what is required. Turning to the case of signature based detection methods the picture is less clear. One detector performs well in one study—and meets expectations—but is much less convincing in another, where it performs on a par with the anomaly-based methods studied. Whether some of the more difficult demands, such as the detection of masqueraders or the detection of novel intrusions, can be met without the use of anomaly-based intrusion detection is still an open question.

It should be noted that the assumptions made above hinge on the *operator's* ability to deal with false alarms. Studies in psychology indicate that humans are typically ill equipped to effectively supervise complex systems in an environment where the monitoring systems produce alarms that turn out not to be real causes for concern [RDL87, WH99]. These result indicate that the more complex the system, and the less the human feels aware of *how* the system is operating (i.e. to what degree it seems 'automagical') the less effective the operator becomes in correctly identifying problematic situations and taking the necessary corrective action. The results seem remarkably stable regardless of the type of system under study, whether in the process industry (paper mill, steel mill, aluminum smelting facility etc.) [RDL87], or air craft cockpit or nuclear power plant control room [WH99].

Thus it is reasonable to assume that if we cannot reduce the false alarm rate of current intrusion detection systems, it would be beneficial to provide the operator with tools to help her address them, i.e. by identifying them, discarding them, and ultimately correcting the intrusion detection system that produced them. This will in effect provide the operator with more insight into how the intrusion detection system is operating. Thus Chapter 3 provides the rationale for addressing the false alarm problem.

5.1 Chapter 4: Visualizing Intrusions: Watching the Webserver

Following the rationale in the previous chapter, applying visualization to the output of a traditional anomaly based intrusion detection system could help the operator make sense of the output. The aim is to help the operator differentiate false alarms from the true alarms. This could combine advantages of both methods while mitigating their drawbacks, namely:

Anomaly detection advantage: being able to detect novel intrusions, i.e. previously undetected and unknown methods of intrusion; disadvantages: having a high false alarm rate as consequence of detecting unusual behavior instead of just known violations.

Visualization advantage: increasing the operator's insight into the data being presented; disadvantage: not being able to display the typically large amounts of data that intrusion detection systems deal with in a meaningful way.

To this end, we describe how a very simple anomaly detection based log reduction system with a 3D visualization component was applied to the realistically sized log of a web server. The log was from the month of November of 2002 and came from the webserver of the Computer Science Department at Chalmers. It contained around 1.2 million accesses, comprised of about 220000 unique access requests.

We describe an anomaly based log reduction scheme which works by cutting up the unique requests into elements as per the HTTP specification, and then counting the frequencies of occurrences of the elements, assigning a score to the request as a whole by calculating the average of the element scores. A low score signifies that the request was comprised of *unusual* elements, and hence anomalous in some sense. It should be noted that the element frequencies were maximized at a frequency of 1000, so as to prevent a small set very frequent elements from completely dominating the score of those access requests of which they were part. The cut-off score was motivated visually. When applying an anomaly based intrusion detection system it would be typical to settle on a threshold score and to mark all the requests with a lower score as anomalous. However, instead we choose as many of the lowest scoring access requests as we can handle with the visualization component, irrespective of their score. So strictly speaking we in fact implement an anomaly detection based log reduction scheme.

The visualization component then performed the same separation into elements as the log reducer, but instead visualized the elements as a general graph, with directed edges connecting the elements. I.e. given an access request such as "GET /index.html HTTP/1.0", it would first be cut up into the nodes: "GET", "index.html", "HTTP" and "1.0", and then the edges between "GET" and "index.html" etc. would be added. Note that the resulting graph is a general graph (e.g. not necessarily acyclic etc.), where a node may be a part of several access requests at different places. The resulting (mostly treelike) structure was visualized as a 3D graph and even while the first feature that stood out turned out to be an attack, later investigation indicated that the visualization was better suited to help identify benign requests than malicious requests. This was just as well, as the majority of the log was comprised of benign access requests. Even though a direct comparison between the false alarm rates defined in Chapter 3 and the results in this chapter was impossible, the false alarm rate was orders of magnitude worse than required in Chapter 3 but the visualization component was effective in helping the operator identifying the false alarms and hence by a process of elimination, the true alarms.

Many interesting attempted intrusions were found in the data and were divided into some seven classes. While the log reduction scheme did not have a perfect detection rate, it did not miss any one class completely, so evidence of all *types* of attacks was preserved. To ascertain the detection rate, all the 220000 access requests were classified by hand, an *extremely* tedious task.

Chapter 5: Combining a Bayesian Classifier with Visualization: Understanding the IDS

While the method that is presented in Chapter 4 is workable it does have some drawbacks. The main drawback pertains to the log reduction scheme. While it works as it stands, it does so without lending the user any real insight into its operation, the graphs motivating the cut off frequencies notwithstanding. Furthermore, it cannot be configured by the user, should e.g. the visualization component have given any insight into how its performance could be improved. Also it is a pure anomaly based system and (as we discuss in Section 2.4) for better detection accuracy an intrusion detection system ought to have a model of both benign and malicious behavior.

An anecdote from the chapter serves to motivate the approach taken:

> When the author first started using the Bayesian spam filter recently added to the *Mozilla* ("http://www.mozilla.org") email client, the filter seemed to learn the difference between spam and non-spam email with surprisingly little training. It was not until some rather important email was misclassified as 'spam' that it was realized that what the filter had actually learnt, was not the difference between spam and non-spam, but between messages written in English and the author's native tongue. In fairness given a few more benign examples of English messages the system was successfully retrained and was again correctly classifying email, but some rudimentary insight into exactly what the system had learnt would have made us more skeptical of the quality of the classification, even though the classifier seemed to operate perfectly judging by the output.

To attempt to address this situation, a naive Bayesian classifier was developed. It was modeled after the now common spam filters first popularized by Paul Graham [Gra02]. The main reasons for this choice was that these classifiers have had some success in the similar field of spam detection and they also meet the requirement that they build a complete model given the available evidence, taking both benign and malicious clues into account. In fact the classifier cannot operate *without* both benign and malicious examples. In order to explain how the visualization of the classifier works we will first have to go into a bit more detail explaining how the classifier actually operates. Naive Bayesian classification revolves around a scenario where that which we wish to classify can be divided into records (i.e. pieces of mail in the case of spam classification) that can be marked as benign or malicious as a whole. The records must furthermore be divisible into tokens (typically words in the case of spam classification, but also message headers etc). Bootstrapping the classifier consist of feeding it records the user has marked as either benign or malicious. The principle behind the classifier is thus one of *directed self learning*. In more detail, the classifier operates by counting the frequencies of occurrence of the tokens that makes up the good and bad records. The frequency counts for each token can be interpreted (by the application of some conversion formula) as a probability indicating the relative maliciousness of the token, i.e. the probability that the token indicates a bad context. Let us call this probability P_l (for *local probability*). The probability that the same token is indicative of a good record is then of course simply $1 - P_l$. In order to classify a previously unseen record the classifier weighs together the evidence provided by the local probabilities of the tokens that makes up the record, using a neutral 0.5 probability if the token has not been seen previously. This result in a total probability for the record as a whole that can be interpreted analogously with the local probability. The weighing is performed by a naive version of the Bayesian chain rule. As the local probabilities do not actually take the dependent probabilities of the other tokens into account (as that would lead to a state explosion that would be prohibitively costly in terms of memory and processing resources) the classifier earns the moniker *naive*. It is also worth noting that in order for Bayes's theorem to hold the probabilities taken into account ought to be independent of each other. This restriction is often relaxed in practice.

Given this classifier, one realizes that the learning it does is condensed into the local probabilities. Therefore it was decided to try the heatmap visualization principle. The heatmap visualization works by mapping a continuous variable onto the color wheel. From green via yellow, to red. In this case we map local probability from 0.0 being green to 1.0 being red, with 0.5 indicated by yellow onto the background of the textual representation of the tokens. This provides the operator visual insight into the evidence upon which the classifier is basing its conclusion. In the prototype developed, the records are displayed one to a line with the total score also displayed (heatmapped) to the left of the record. As the resulting visualization can also lend insight into the training process and not merely the output of the classifier once it is trained, a natural step is to make it interactive. The user can mark a record benign or malicious and immediately see the effect this update has on the classifier as a whole through the visualization of the record and other records also visible. To help the user keep track of the training status of the record, a colored marker is placed first on the line to indicate whether this record has been trained as "good" or "bad" (or not part of training at all). In order to aid in training, the operator can sort the display according to training status e.g. to easily identify records that have been trained but still are misclassified. To effect actual detection the operator can import new records and sort on total score, which will single out the records most likely to be indicative of malicious activity.

In order to test the complete prototype, named *Bayesvis*, it was trained on the web server access request data described in Chapter 4. A training strategy of *train until no false positives* was adopted, i.e. the system was first trained on all the previously identified malicious requests and then enough of the benign requests were trained to make all the benign training request have an overall score lower than 0.5, signifying that they are benign. The resulting classifier was then tested on the available logs from the same web server for the months following November, i.e. December through February. While the December log contained on the order of the same number of access requests, many of these were identical to the November log and were removed from it. The same applied for the following logs, i.e. many of the requests in the January log were identical to requests seen in either the November or December logs. Thus the actual logs the classifier was tested on decreased in size as the experiment wore on. The results were promising, the number of false alarms was reasonable and because of the visualization they were quite easily identifiable, as the operator could (the author would argue) see what tokens the classifier found objectionable. An access request consisting of predominantly green tokens with one or two red mixed in (perhaps as arguments to cgi scripts) would almost certainly indicate a false alarm. As the operator has knowledge of the meaning of the actual tokens in context (something the classifier itself is devoid of) she is poised to make a qualitative evaluation of the output of the classifier. The detection capabilities were also sufficient: the detector clearly managed to generalize its evidence from the training session to detect variations of previously known attacks.

Chapter 6: Visualizing the Inner Workings of a Self Learning Classifier: Improving the Usability of Intrusion Detection Systems

A problem with the classifier described in Chapter 5 is that it is simple (simplistic even) in that it neither takes the order nor the context of the tokens into account. While in fairness the naive Bayesian classifier shows sufficient performance on the data with which it was tested, there is data on which it cannot be tested given the above mentioned limitations. Furthermore, as it did not perform flawlessly there is room for improvement.

In order to address these two points a more complex classifier based on two popular spam filters: CRM-114 [Yer04] and Spambayes [MW04] was developed. Our classifier works with the same notions of tokens, records, directed training etc. as the naive Bayesian classifier in Chapter 5. It works by sliding a window of length six over the input and considering as features all the possible subsequences of the tokens in the window considering *skips*, i.e. the order of the tokens is preserved, but they may not be counted as present. E.g. the window "The quick brown fox jumps over", gives rise to (among others) the features "The <skip> <skip> fox jumps over" and "<skip> quick brown fox jumps over", etc. until all possible subsequences have been generated. These features are first processed much as the tokens are in the naive Bayesian classifier, i.e. their presence in benign and malicious contexts are counted and the statistics allowed to influence a local probability. In this case the formula of the local probability is more sophisticated, giving less weight to features for which low counts have been observed (i.e. for which there is less total evidence). However, as this would give equal weight to features that have many tokens present (i.e. few skips) as to features that have fewer tokens present, a superincreasing weight function is applied that modifies the local probabilities according to the formula: $W = 1/2^{2(n-1)}$. I.e. a feature with more tokens present can outweigh all of its "children"—i.e. with skips in the positions that the feature has tokens—combined. This is believed to make the classifier non-linear i.e. a classifier that could e.g. learn that 'A' and 'B' in isolation were both indicative of a malicious context, but 'AB' together was indicative of a good context, something the naive Bayesian classifier could not. Further study is required to confirm whether this scheme could indeed lead to a classifier that is non-linear. So far our classifier has been solely influenced by the CRM-114 classifier.

Given the local probabilities they have to be combined into an overall score indicating the probability the record is indicative of malicious activity much as in Chapter 5. As in the SpamBayes classifier, to accomplish this a chi square test (or rather *two* tests) was applied to the local probabilities. The local probabilities of the features are tested against the two hypotheses of them being indications of benign or malicious behaviour, thus resulting in two probabilities. These are then combined into one probability, taking the support for both hypotheses into account. For the situations where there is either strong evidence of malicious activity and none of benign (or vice versa) the situation is straightforward giving rise to the probability of either 1.0 or 0.0 respectively. The situation where we do not have much evidence of either gives rise to the overall score of 0.5. The special case where we have equal evidence of *both* malicious and benign activity is interesting though, as that must also give rise to the overall score of 0.5, but of course still being a very different situation from the case where we do not have much evidence of either kind. As a result, all three probabilities of the classifier are returned to the application for visualization.

Visualizing this classifier is much more problematic than the naive Bayesian classifier as there are many more features and a more complex decision process to take into account. Since we still deal with probabilities, some form of heatmap could still be applied. But now no single token has a score, and the simple *line per record* display of Bayesvis cannot be applied directly. Thus it was decided to apply the principle of *overview and detail*, whereby the data is displayed in progressively more detail as the user selects various regions of interest.

In order to evaluate the resulting prototype, called *Chi2vis*, it was trained on and applied to the November 2002 log as that had been fully evaluated for benign and malicious accesses. As is customary in classifier research, the system was trained on a randomly chosen ten percent subset from the seven classes of attacks (though at minimum one request) and the benign requests. The classifier was then evaluated on the remaining data for true and false positives and negatives. The resulting detector faired well, and the visualization helped the operator identify false alarms, more so than Bayesvis, in that Chi2vis lets the operator see the (limited) context in which the training took place so that the operator gained extra insight into what the detector found objectionable and why that may not hold in the particular case. Chi2vis was also tested on traces of operating system calls. Unfortunately there was really not enough data available to train Chi2vis sufficiently but it still managed to correctly detect at least some (visually very uninteresting) bad traces, even though the performance of Chi2vis on this data set was not spectacular. To complete the evaluation, Bayesvis was then tested under the same circumstances to make a comparison possible. While Bayesvis required less benign training before the *train until no false positives* strategy was fulfilled, this was reflected in a higher false alarm rate and lower detection work that dealt with web access requests stopped when the *types* of malicious accesses were found the method investigated in this work nicely complements those methods in that with the approach presented here the investigation could continue and the actual entities making the request could be identified.

However, in the version of paper on which the chapter is based, one malicious pattern slipped by. This was because the pattern consisted of two separate unique access request strings and only a few accesses overall and was therefore similar to the benign traffic to the web server. This pattern turned out to be from the same tool as mentioned in the previous paragraph, but run with different options. The reason for this pattern escaping the author the first time around is illustrative as it makes the main drawback of all visualization work clear: any visualization can only be as successful as the person viewing it. If that person falters thorough inattentiveness (perhaps brought on by tiredness, stress or boredom for example) then the visualization cannot ameliorate the situation. Putting the human operator back into the driver's seat, so to speak, has both the benefit of putting the human in control of the events, but also the drawback of having to come to terms with human fallibility.

rate. Bayesvis faired almost universally worse on all aspects in comparison to Chi2vis.

Chapter 7: Visualization for Intrusion Detection: Hooking the worm.

This chapter is based on our first foray in the field of applying visualization to intrusion detection[Axe03]. Access requests (in this case the complete records, not just the unique request strings) to a small personal web server are studied with a visualization method called the *parallel coordinate plot* [Ins97]. The hypothesis here is that the operator should be able to detect malicious accesses to the webserver—most notably from the various *worms* that bounce around the internet—and be able to correlate them to each other. It should be noted that the web server in this case was much smaller than the ones studied in the previously summarized chapters, and did not have nearly the same number of accesses to it. It furthermore did not have much in the way of benign access requests. Further complicating the study of this web server, it used authentication for all accesses and hence all worms trying to access it got an error return. To accomplish the detection and classification of the worms (and other entities) that accessed the server, a selection of variables that did not leak information (directly or indirectly) about the authentication process was visualized using the parallel coordinate plot. The parallel coordinate plot maps a point in multidimensional space onto the plane by placing all the axes vertically and equidistant and plotting the components of the point onto each respective axis, connecting the components with straight line segments. The detection and identification was achieved via a trellis plot, i.e. one of the variables (the unique access request string as in the previous chapters) was held constant and a separate parallel coordinate plot generated for each unique access request. This meant that the patterns of access for the various unique request strings could be visually correlated to each other, i.e. entities making different requests but at similar times, from similar systems etc. could be identified and the access requests correlated.

Relatively little support for the hypothesis that malicious entities could be detected was found. While many of the worms showed markedly different access patterns from the benign patterns it is difficult to say how that would hold up given a larger web site with more benign traffic. The malicious access requests (and the benign) could be successfully correlated to each other though. In fact, one entity making access requests very similar to then popular worms was markedly different visually and turned out to be a then largely unknown instance of the application of a tool for breaking into web sites. Most security sources erroneously referred to this access request as coming from the worm. The visualization made it easy to differentiate this access pattern from the others. Several other malicious access patterns were found. As the previous

Chapter 2

AN INTRODUCTION TO
INTRUSION DETECTION

1. Intrusion Prevention

Several methods are available to protect a computer system or network from attack. A good introduction to such methods is [HB95], from which this section borrows heavily. The paper lists six general, non-exclusive approaches to anti-intrusion techniques: pre-emption, prevention, deterrence, detection deflection, and countermeasures (see Figure 2.1):

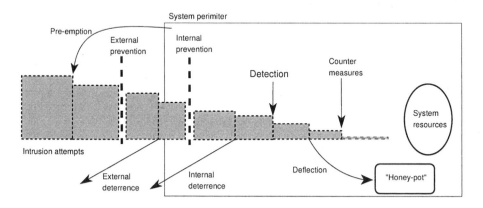

Figure 2.1. Anti-intrusion techniques (from [HB95])

1 *Pre-emption* To strike against the threat before it has had a chance to mount its attack, in the spirit of: "Do unto others, before they do unto you." In a civilian setting, this is a dangerous and possibly unlawful approach, where innocent—and indeed not so innocent—bystanders may be harmed.

2 *Prevention* To preclude or severely limit the likelihood of a particular intrusion succeeding. One can, for example, elect to not be connected to the Internet if one is afraid of being attacked by that route, or choose to be connected via some restriction mechanism such as a firewall. Proving your software free of security defects also falls under this heading. Unfortunately, this can be an expensive and awkward approach, since it is easy to throw the baby out with the bath water in the attempt to prevent attacks. Internal prevention comes under the control of the system owner, while external prevention takes place in the environment surrounding the system, such as a larger organization, or society as a whole.

3 *Deterrence* To persuade an attacker to hold off his attack, or to break off an ongoing attack. Typically this is accomplished by increasing the perceived risk of negative consequences for the attacker. Of course, if the value of the protected resource is great, the determined attacker may not be scared off so easily. Internal deterrence can take the form of login banners warning potential internal and external attackers of dire consequences should they proceed. External deterrence could be effected by the legal system, with laws against computer crime and the strict enforcement of the same.

4 *Detection* To identify intrusion attempts, so that the proper response can be evoked. This most often takes the form of notifying the proper authority. The problems are obvious: the difficulty of defending against a hit-and-run attack, and the problem of false alarms, or failing to sound the alarm when someone surreptitiously gains, or attempts to gain, access.

5 *Deflection* To lure an intruder into thinking that he has succeeded when in fact he has been herded away from areas where he could do real damage. The main problem is that of managing to fool an experienced attacker, at least for a sufficient period of time.

6 *Countermeasures* To counter actively and autonomously an intrusion while it is in progress. This can be done without the need for detection, since the countermeasure does not have to discriminate—although it is preferable if it can—between a legitimate user who makes a mistake and an intruder who sets off a predetermined response, or "booby trap".

The reasons for our desire to employ the principle of surveillance are much the same as in the physical security arena: we wish to deploy a defence in depth; we do not believe in the infallibility of the perimeter defence; when someone manages to slip through or even attempts to attack we do not want them to have undetected free reign of the system; for technical reasons we perhaps cannot strengthen our perimeter defences (lack of source code etc.); we wish to defend not only against outsiders, but also against insiders, those that already operate within the perimeter, etc.

2. Intrusion Detection

As the principle of surveillance stems from the application of intrusion detection systems to computer security it is fitting to start with a few definitions and introduction to that area of study. Research in intrusion detection is the study of systems that automatically detect intrusions into computer systems. They are designed to detect computer security violations made by the following important types of attackers:

- Attackers using prepackaged exploit scripts. Primarily outsiders.

- Automated attacks originating from other computers, so called *worms*.

- Attackers operating under the identity of a legitimate user, for example by having stolen that user's authentication information (password). Outsiders and insiders.

- Insiders abusing legitimate privileges, etc.

Giving satisfactory definitions to there terms turns out to be problematic. Although most computer users could easily describe what they do not want to happen with their computers, finding strict definitions of these actions is often surprisingly difficult. Furthermore, many security problems arise between the ordinary every day definitions that we use to communicate security, and the strict definitions that are necessary to research. For example the simple phrase "Alice speaks to Bob on the freshly authenticated channel" is very difficult to interpret in a packet-sending context, and indeed severe security problems have arisen from confusion arising from the application of such simple models such as "speaking" in a computer communications context [Gol00]. That numerous, spectacular mistakes have been made by computer security researchers and professionals only serves to demonstrate the difficulty of the subject.

2.1 Definitions

That said, a definition of what we mean by *intrusion* and other related terms remains essential, at least in the context of *intrusion detection*:

Intrusion The *malicious* violation of a *security policy* (implied or otherwise) by an *unauthorized agent*.

Intrusion detection The automated detection and alarm of any situation where an intrusion has taken, or is about to take place. (The detection must be complemented with an alert to the proper authority if it is to act as a useful security measure.)

We will consider these definitions in greater detail in the following paragraphs:

Malicious. The person who breaks into or otherwise unduly influences our computer system is deemed not have our best interests at heart. This is an interesting point, for in general it is impossible for the intrusion detection system to decide whether the agent of the security violation has malicious intent or not, even after the fact. Thus we may expect the intrusion detection system to raise the alarm whenever there is sufficient evidence of an activity that *could* be motivated by malice. By this definition this will result in a false alarm, but in most cases a benign one, since most people do not mind the alarm being raised about a potentially dangerous situation that has arisen from human error rather than malicious activity.

Security Policy. This stresses that the violations against which we wish to protect are, to a large extent, in the eyes of the owner of the resource being protected (in western law at least). Other legitimate demands on security may in future be made by the state legislature. Some branches of the armed services are already under such obligations, but in the civilian sector few (if any) such demands are currently made. In practice security policies are often weak, however, and in a civilian setting we often do not know what to classify as a violation until after the fact. Thus it is beneficial if our intrusion detection system can operate in circumstances where the security policy is weakly defined, or even non-existent. One way of circumventing this inherent problem is for the supplier of the intrusion detection system to define a *de facto* security policy that contains elements with which she hopes all users of her system will agree. This situation may be compared with the law of the land, only a true subset of which is agreed by most citizens to define *real* criminal acts. It goes without saying that a proper security policy is preferable. This ought to be defined as the set of actions (or rather principles) of operation that are allowed, instead of in the negative for best security.

Unauthorized Agent. The definition is framed to address the threat that comes from an *unauthorized agent*, and should not be interpreted too narrowly. The term singles out all those who are not legitimate owners of the system, i.e., who are not allowed to make decisions that affect the security policy. This does not specifically exclude *insiders* i.e. people who are authorized to use the system to a greater or lesser extent, but not authorized to perform all possible actions. The point of this distinction is that we do not attempt to encompass those violations that would amount to protecting the owner from himself. To accomplish this is, of course, both simple and impossible: simple in the sense that if the owner makes a simple legitimate mistake, a timely warning may make him see his error and take corrective action; impossible, in that if the person who legally commands the system wishes to destroy or otherwise influence the system, there is no way to prevent him, short of taking control of the system away from him, in which case he no longer "legally commands the system." When all is said and done, trust has to be placed in an entity, and our only defense against this trust being abused is to use risk management activities external to the intrusion detection system. It is a difficult question as to whether we should consider non-human attackers such as other computers to be agents in themselves, or merely tools acting on the behalf of some other agent. We will not delve more deeply into such questions here.

Automated Detection and Alarm. The research into intrusion detection has almost exclusively considered systems that operate largely without human supervision. An interesting class of systems that has not been studied to any significant degree (the present book excepted) are those that operate with a larger degree of human supervision, placing so much responsibility on the human operator that *she* can be thought of as the detection element proper (or at least a significant part of it). Such systems would support the human in observing and making decisions about the security state of the supervised system; a 'security camera' for computer systems. Continued reliance solely on fully automated systems may turn out to be less than optimal.

Delivered to the Proper Authority. It cannot be overemphasized that the alarm must be *delivered* to the *proper authority*—henceforth referred to as the Site Security Officer or SSO—in such a manner that the SSO can take action. The ubiquitous car alarm today arouses little, if any, response from the public, and hence does not act as an effective deterrent to would-be car thieves. Thus the SSO's response, which may or may not be aided by automatic systems within the intrusion detection system itself, is a crucial component in the fielding of intrusion detection systems. There has been little research, even in the simpler field of automated alarms, into how to present information to the SSO so that she can make the correct decision and take the correct action. It is important that the authority that is expected to take corrective action in the face of computer security violations—keeping in mind that such violations often originate "in house"—really *has* the authority to take the appropriate action. This is not always the case in a civilian setting.

Intrusion has Taken Place. The phrase "any situation where an *intrusion has taken place*" may seem self-evident. However, there are important questions over the exact moment when the intrusion detection system *can* detect the intrusion. It is clearly impossible in the general case to sound the alarm when mere intent is present. There is a better chance of raising the alarm when preparatory action is taking place, while the best chance comes when a bona fide violation has taken place, or is ongoing. The case where we consider an intrusion which is "about to take place" is interesting enough to warrant special treatment. In military circles this falls under the heading of *indication and warning*; there are sufficient signs that something is imminent to ensure that our level of readiness is affected. In a computer security context, the study of such clues, many of which are of course not "technological" in nature, is not far advanced. It is an important subject, however, since it actually gives us the opportunity to ward off or otherwise hinder an attack. Without such possibilities, an alarm can only help to reduce the damage after the fact, or can only function as a deterrent.

2.2   Intrusion Detection Systems

The study of intrusion detection is today some twenty five years old. The possibility of automatic intrusion detection was first put forward in James Anderson's classic paper [And80], in which he states that a certain class of intruders—the so-called *masqueraders*, or intruders who operate with stolen identities—could probably be detected by their departures from the set norm for the original user. Later the idea of checking all activities against a set security policy was introduced.

We can group intrusion detection systems into two overall classes: those that detect anomalies, hereafter termed *anomaly detection systems*, and those that detect the signatures of known attacks, hereafter termed *signature based systems*. Often the former automatically forms an opinion on what is 'normal' for the system, for example by constructing a profile of the commands issued by each user and then sounding the alarm when the subject deviates sufficiently from the norm. Signature systems, on the other hand, are most often programmed beforehand to detect the signatures of intrusions known of in advance.

These two techniques are still with us today, and with the exception of hybrid approaches nothing essentially new has been put forward in this area. Section 2.4 will explain these two approaches in terms of detection and estimation theory.

2.3   An Architectural Model of Intrusion Detection Systems

Since the publication of Anderson's seminal paper [And80], several intrusion detection systems have been invented. Today there exists a sufficient number of systems in the field for one to be able to form some sort of notion of a 'typical' intrusion detection system, and its constituent parts. Figure 2.2 depicts such a system. Please note that not all possible data/control flows have been included in the figure, but only the most important ones.

Any generalised architectural model of an intrusion detection system would contain at least the following elements:

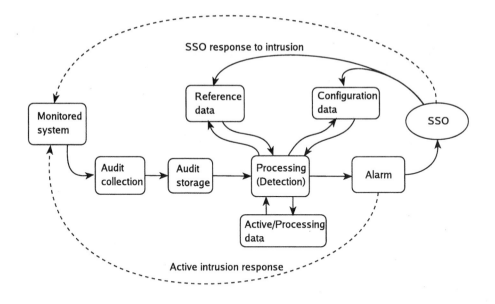

Figure 2.2. Organisation of a generalised intrusion detection system

Audit collection Audit data must be collected on which to base intrusion detection decisions. Many different parts of the monitored system can be used as sources of data: keyboard input, command based logs, application based logs, etc. In most cases network activity or host-based security logs, or both, are used.

Audit storage Typically, the audit data is stored somewhere, either indefinitely[1] for later reference, or temporarily awaiting processing. The volume of data is often exceedingly large[2], making this is a crucial element in any intrusion detection system, and leading some researchers to view intrusion detection as a problem in audit data reduction [Fra94, ALGJ98]

Processing The processing block is the heart of the intrusion detection system. It is here that one or many algorithms are executed to find evidence (with some degree of certainty) in the audit trail of suspicious behavior. More will be said about the detector proper in Section 2.4.

Configuration data This is the state that affects the operation of the intrusion detection system: how and where to collect audit data, how to respond

---

[1]Or at least for a long time—perhaps several months or years—compared to the processing turn around time.
[2]The problem of collecting sufficient but not excessive amounts of audit data has been described as "You either die of thirst, or you are allowed a drink from a fire hose."

to intrusions, etc. This is therefore the SSO's main means of controlling the intrusion detection system. This data can grow surprisingly large and complex in a real world intrusion detection installation. Furthermore, it is relatively sensitive, since access to this data would give the competent intruder information on which avenues of attack are likely to go undetected.

Reference data The reference data storage stores information about known intrusion signatures—for misuse systems—or profiles of normal behavior—for anomaly systems. In the latter case the processing element updates the profiles as new knowledge about the observed behavior becomes available. This update is often performed at regular intervals in batches. Stored intrusion signatures are most often updated by the SSO, as and when new intrusion signatures become known. The analysis of novel intrusions is a highly skilled task. More often than not, the only realistic mode for operating the intrusion detection system is one where the SSO subscribes to some outside source of intrusion signatures. At present these are proprietary. In practice it is difficult, if not impossible, to make intrusion detection systems operate with signatures from an alternate source, even though it is technically feasible [LMPT98].

Active/processing data The processing element must frequently store intermediate results, for example information about partially fulfilled intrusion signatures. The space needed to store this active data can grow quite large.

Alarm This part of the system handles all output from the system, whether it be an automated response to suspicious activity, or more commonly the notification of a SSO.

2.4   Explaining Intrusion Detection From the Perspective of Detection and Estimation Theory[4]

Research into the automated detection of computer security violations is hardly in its infancy, yet little comparison has been made with the established field of detection and estimation theory (one exception being [LMS00]) the results of which have been found applicable to a wide range of problems in other disciplines. In order to explain the two major approaches behind intrusion detection principles we will attempt such a comparison, studying the problem of intrusion detection by the use of the introductory models of detection and estimation theory.

---

[4]This section is based on [Axe00b].

Classical Detection Theory

The problem of detecting a signal transmitted over a noisy channel is one of great technical importance, and has consequently been studied thoroughly for some time now. An introduction to detection and estimation theory is given in [Tre68], from which this section borrows heavily.

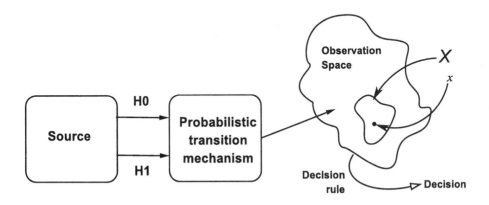

Figure 2.3. Classical detection theory model

In classical binary detection theory (see Figure 2.3) we should envisage a system that consists of a source from which originates one of two signals, *H0* or *H1*, for *hypothesis zero* and *one* respectively. This signal is transmitted via some channel that invariably adds noise and distorts the signal according to a probabilistic transition mechanism. The output—what we receive—can be described as a point in a finite (multidimensional) observation space, for example x in Figure 2.3. Since this is a problem that has been studied by statisticians for some time, we have termed it the *classical detection model*. Based on an observation of the output of the source as transmitted through the probabilistic transition mechanism, we arrive at a decision. Our decision is based on a decision rule; for example: 'Is or is not x in X,' where X is the region in the observation space that defines the set of observations that we believe to be indicative of *H0* (or *H1*) (see Figure 2.3). We then make a decision as to whether the source sent *H0* or *H1* based on the outcome of the comparison of x and X.

Note that the source and signal model *H0* and *H1* could represent any of a number of interesting problems, and not only the case of transmitting a one or a zero. For example, *H1* could represent the presence of a disease (and conversely *H0* its absence), and the observation space could be any number of measurable physiological parameters such as blood count. The decision would then be one of 'sick' or 'healthy.' In our case it would be natural to assign the symbol *H1* to some form of intrusive activity, and *H0* to its absence.

The problem is then one of deciding the nature of the probabilistic transition mechanism. We must choose what data should be part of our observation space, and on this basis derive a decision rule that maximizes the detection rate and minimizes the false alarm rate, or settle for some desirable combination of the two.

When deciding on the decision rule the *Bayes criterion* is a useful measurement of success [Tre68, pp. 24]. In order to conduct a Bayes test, we must first know the a priori probabilities of the source output (see Chapter 3 for further discussion). Let us call these P_0 and P_1 for the probability of the source sending a zero or a one respectively. Second, we assign a cost to each of the four possible courses of action. These costs are named C_{00}, C_{10}, C_{11}, and C_{01}, where the first subscript indicates the output from our decision rule—what we though had been sent—and the second what was actually sent. Each decision or experiment then incurs a cost, in as much as we can assign a cost or value to the different outcomes. For example, in the intrusion detection context, the detection of a particular intrusion could potentially save us an amount that can be deduced from the potential cost of the losses if the intrusion had gone undetected. We aim to design our decision rule so that the *average* cost will be minimized. The expected value—R for *risk*—of the cost is then [Tre68, p. 9]:

$$
\begin{aligned}
R = &C_{00}P_0P(\text{say } H0|H0 \text{ is true}) \\
&+C_{10}P_0P(\text{say } H1|H0 \text{ is true}) \\
&+C_{11}P_1P(\text{say } H1|H1 \text{ is true}) \\
&+C_{01}P_1P(\text{say } H0|H1 \text{ is true})
\end{aligned}
\tag{2.1}
$$

It is natural to assume that $C_{10} > C_{00}$ and $C_{01} > C_{11}$, in other words the cost associated with an incorrect decision or misjudgment is higher than that of a correct decision. Given knowledge of the a priori possibilities and a choice of C parameter values, we can then construct a Bayes optimal detector.

Though Figure 2.3 may lead one to believe that this is a multidimensional problem, it can be shown [Tre68, p. 29] that a *sufficient statistic* can always be found whereby a coordinate transform from our original problem results in a new point that has the property that only one of its coordinates contains all the information necessary for making the detection decision. Figure 2.4 depicts such a case, where the only important parameter of the original multidimensional problem is named *L*.

It can furthermore be shown that the two main approaches to maximizing the desirable properties of the detection—the Bayes or Neyman-Pearson criteria—amount to the same thing; the detector finds a likelihood ratio (which will be a function only of the sufficient statistic above) and then compares this ratio with

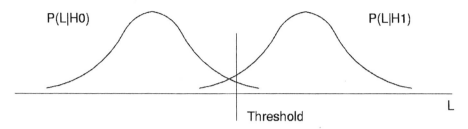

Figure 2.4. One dimensional detection model

a pre-set threshold. By varying the threshold in Figure 2.4, it can be seen that the detection ratio (where we correctly say *H1*) and the false alarm rate (where we incorrectly say *H1*) will vary in a predictable manner. Hence, if we have complete knowledge of the probability densities of *H0* and *H1* we can construct an optimal detector, or at least calculate the properties of such a detector. We will later apply this theory to explain anomaly and signature detection.

Application to the Intrusion Detection Problem

This section is a discussion of the way in which the intrusion detection problem may be explained in light of the classical model described above.

Source Starting with the *source*, ours is different from that of the ordinary radio transmitter because it is human in origin. Our source is a human computer user who issues commands to the computer system using any of a number of input devices. In the vast majority of cases, the user is benevolent and non-malicious, and he is engaged solely in non-intrusive activity. The user sends only *H0*, that is, non-intrusive activity. Even when the user is malicious, his activity will still mostly consist of benevolent activity. Some of his activity will however be malicious, that is, he will send *H1*. Note that *malicious* has to be interpreted liberally, and can arise from a number of different types of activities such as those described by the taxonomies in for example [LBMC94, LJ97]. Thus, for example, the use of a pre-packed exploit script is one such source of intrusive activity. A *masquerading*[5] intruder can be another source of intrusive activity. In this case the activity that he initiates differs from the activity that the proper user would have originated.

It should be noted that we have only treated the binary case here, differentiating between 'normal' behavior and one type of intrusion. In reality there are many different types of intrusions, and different detectors are needed to detect

---

[5]A *masquerader* is an intruder that operates under false identity. The term was first used by Anderson in [And80].

them. Thus the problem is really a multi-valued problem, that is, in an operational context we must differentiate between *H0* and *H1, H2, H3...,* where *H1–Hn* are different types of intrusions. To be able to discriminate between these different types of intrusions, some statistical difference between a parameter in the *H0* and *H1* situation must be observable. This is simple, almost trivial, in some cases, but difficult in others where the observed behavior is similar to benevolent behavior. Knowledge, even if incomplete, of the statistical properties of the 'signals' that are sent is crucial to make the correct detection decision.

It should be noted that earlier classifications of computer security violations that exist [LBMC94, NP89, LJ97] are not directed at intrusion detection, and on closer study appear to be formulated on too high a level of representation to be directly applicable to the problem in hand. There are now a handful of studies that links the classification of different computer security violations to the problem of detection, in this case the problem of what traces are necessary to detect intrusions after the fact [ALGJ98, Bar04a, KMT04, Max03].

Probabilistic Transition Mechanism In order to detect intrusive behavior we have first to observe it. In a computer system context it is rare to have the luxury of observing user behavior directly, looking over the user's shoulder while he provides a running commentary on what he is doing and intends to do. Instead we have to observe the user by other means, often by some sort of security logging mechanism, although it is also possible by observing the network traffic emanating from the user. Other more direct means have also been proposed, such as monitoring the user's keystrokes.

In the usual application of detection theory, the probabilistic transition mechanism, or "channel", often adds noise of varying magnitude to the signal. This noise can be modeled and incorporated into the overall model of the transmission system. The same applies to the intrusion detection case, although our "noise" is of a different nature and does not in general arise from nature, as described by physics. In our case we observe the subject by some (imperfect) means where several sources of noise can be identified. One such source is where other users' behavior is mixed with that of the user under study, and it is difficult to identify the signal we are interested in.

If, for example, our user proves to be malicious, and sends TCP-syn packets from a PC connected to a network of PCs to a target host, intended to execute a SYN-flooding denial-of-service attack on that host. Since the source host is on a network of PCs—the operating systems of which are known to suffer from flaws that make them prone to sending packet storms that look like SYN-flooding attacks to the uninitiated[6]—it may be difficult to detect the malicious

---

[6]Or at least *were* prone to ten years ago.

user. This is because he operates from under the cover of the noise added by the poorly implemented TCP/IP stacks of the computers on the same source network. It can thus be much more difficult to build a model of our 'channel' than when the noise arises as a result of a purely physical process.

Observation Space   Given that the action has taken place, and that it has been 'transmitted' through the logging system/channel, we can make observations. The set of possible observations, given a particular source and channel model, makes up our *observation space*. As said earlier, some results suggest that we can always make some sort of coordinate transformation that transforms all available information into one coordinate in the observation space. Thus in every detection situation we need to find this transform.

In most cases the computer security we are presented with will be discrete in nature, not continuous. This is different from the common case in detection theory where the signals are most often continuous in nature. In our case a record from a host-based security log will contain information such as commands or system calls that were executed, who initiated them, any arguments such as files read, written to, or executed, what permissions were utilized to execute the operation, and whether it succeeded or not. In the case of network data we will typically not have such high quality since the data may not contain all security relevant information; for example, we will not know exactly how the attacked system will respond to the data that it is sent, or whether the requested operation succeeded or not [PN98]. The question of what data to log in order to detect intrusions of varying kinds is central, but for a long time this question was largely unaddressed. We also know little of the way different intrusions manifest themselves when logged by different means.

Once again the literature is hardly extensive, although for example [ALGJ98, HL93, LB98] and more recently [Bar04b] have addressed the issues presented in this section, albeit from different angles.

Decision Rule   Having made the coordinate transformation in the previous step we then need to decide on a threshold to distinguish between *H0* and *H1*.

Thus our hope when we apply anomaly detection is that all that is not normal behavior for the source in question—that cannot be construed as *H0*—is some sort of intrusive behavior. The question is thus to what degree abnormal equates to intrusive. This is perhaps most likely in the case of a *masquerader* who one may presume is not trained to emulate the user whose identity he has assumed. There are some studies that suggest that different users indeed display sufficiently different behavior for them to be told apart [LB98].

Existing Approaches to Intrusion Detection

For a survey of existing approaches to intrusion detection see [BAJ03]. Here we will only outline the two major methods of intrusion detection: *anomaly detection* and *signature detection*. These have been with us since the inception of the field. In short, *anomaly detection* can be defined as looking for the unexpected—that which is unusual is suspect—at which point the alarm should be raised. *Signature detection*, on the other hand, relies on the explicit codifying of 'illegal' behavior, and when traces of such behavior is found the alarm is raised.

Anomaly Detection Taking the basic outline of detection and estimation theory laid out in the beginning of this section, we can elaborate upon it in describing these methods. In contrast to the model in Figure 2.4, where we have knowledge of both *H0* and *H1*, here we operate without any knowledge of *H1*. Thus we choose a region in our observation space—X in Figure 2.3. To do so, we must transform the observed, normal behavior in such a manner that it makes sense in our observation space context. The region X will contain the transformed normal behavior, and typically also behavior that is 'close' to it, in such a way as to provide some leeway in the decision, trading off some of the detection rate to lower the false alarm rate. The detector proper then flags all occurrences of x in X as no alarm, and all occurrences of x *not* in X as an alarm. Note that X may be a disjoint region in the observation space.

Signature Detection The signature detector detects evidence of intrusive activity irrespective of the model of the background traffic; these detectors have to be able to operate no matter what the background traffic, looking instead for patterns or signals that are thought by the designers to stand out against any possible background traffic. Thus we choose a region in our observation space, but in this instance we are only interested in known intrusive behavior. Thus X will here only encompass observations that we believe stem from intrusive behavior plus the same leeway as before, in this case trading off some of the false alarm rate to gain a greater detection rate in the face of 'modified' attacks. During detector operation we flag all occurrences of x in X as an alarm, and all other cases as no alarm. X here may also consist of several disjoint regions, of course.

Comparison with Bayes Optimal Detectors It is an open question to what degree detectors in these classes can be made to, or are, approximate Bayes optimal detectors. In the case of non-parametric intrusion detectors— detectors where we cannot trade off detection rate for false alarm rate by varying some parameter of the detector—merely studying the receiver operating characteristics (ROC) curve cannot give us any clue as to the similarity to a Bayes optimal detector. This is because the ROC curve in this case only contains one point, and it is impossible to ascertain the degree to which the resulting curve follows the optimal Bayes optimal detector. (See Chapter 3for a brief introduction to ROC curves, and [Tre68] for a thorough treatment).

Summary

The dichotomy between *anomaly detection* and *signature detection* that is present in the intrusion detection field, vanishes (or is at least weakened) when we study the problem from the perspective of classical detection theory. If we wish to classify our source behavior correctly as either *H0* or *H1*, knowledge of both distributions of behavior will help us greatly when making the intrusion detection decision. Interestingly, early on only few research prototype took this view [Lee99, BAJ03]; all others were firmly entrenched in either the *H0* or *H1* camp. It may be that further study of this class of detectors will yield more accurate detectors, especially in the face of attackers who try to modify their behavior to escape detection. A detector that operates with a strong source model, taking both *H0* and *H1* behavior into account, will most probably be better able to qualify its decisions by stating strongly that this behavior is not only known to occur in relation to certain intrusions, and further is not a known benign or common occurrence in the supervised system.

The detectors we have developed in connection with this book (except for the one in Chapter 4) all take both *H0* and *H1* into account.

Chapter 3

THE BASE-RATE FALLACY AND
THE DIFFICULTY OF
INTRUSION DETECTION

Many different demands can be made of intrusion detection systems.[1] An important requirement of an intrusion detection system is that it be *effective* i.e. that it should detect a substantial percentage of intrusions into the supervised system, while still keeping the *false alarm* rate at an acceptable level.

This chapter aims to demonstrate that, for a reasonable set of assumptions, the false alarm rate is the limiting factor for the performance of an intrusion detection system. This is due to the base-rate fallacy phenomenon, that in order to achieve substantial values of the Bayesian detection rate, $P(Intrusion|Alarm)$, we have to achieve a—perhaps in some cases unattainably—low false alarm rate.

A selection of reports of intrusion detection performance are reviewed, and the conclusion is reached that there are indications that at least some types of intrusion detection have far to go before they can attain such low false alarm rates.

Many demands can be made of an intrusion detection system (IDS for short) such as *effectiveness, efficiency, ease of use, security, inter-operability, transparency* etc. Although much research has been done in the field in the past ten years, the theoretical limits of many of these parameters have not been studied to any significant degree. The aim of this paper is to discuss one serious problem with regard to the *effectiveness* parameter, especially how the base-rate fallacy may affect the operational effectiveness of an intrusion detection system.

---

[1]This Chapter is based on [Axe00a]

1.   Problems in Intrusion Detection

At present, the many fundamental questions regarding intrusion detection remain largely unanswered. They include, but are by no means limited to:

Effectiveness How effective is the intrusion detection? To what degree does it detect intrusions into the target system, and how good is it at rejecting false positives, so called false alarms?

Ease of use How easy is it to field and operate for a user who is not a security expert, and can such a user add new intrusion scenarios to the system? An important issue in *ease of use* is the question of what demands can be made of the person responding to the intrusion alarm. How high a false alarm rate can she realistically be expected to cope with, and under what circumstances is she likely to ignore an alarm? (It has long been known in security circles that ordinary electronic alarm systems should be circumvented during normal operation of the facility, when supervisory staff are more likely to be lax because they are accustomed to false alarms [Pie48]).

Security When ever more intrusion detection systems are fielded, one would expect ever more attacks directed at the intrusion detection system itself, to circumvent it or otherwise render the detection ineffective. What is the nature of these attacks, and how resilient is the intrusion detection system to them? When the paper this chapter was based on was first published, this question had seen little to no study. Today this problem is more at the forefront of the research and we have begun to address it.

Transparency How intrusive is the fielding of the intrusion detection system to the organization employing it? How many resources will it consume in terms of manpower, etc?

This chapter is concerned with one aspect of one of the questions above, that of *effectiveness*. More specifically it addresses the way in which the base-rate fallacy affects the required performance of the intrusion detection system with regard to false alarm rejection.

2.   The Base-Rate Fallacy

The base-rate fallacy[2] is one of the cornerstones of Bayesian statistics, stemming as it does directly from Bayes's famous theorem that states the relationship between a conditional probability and its opposite, i.e. with the condition transposed:

---

[2] The idea behind this approach stems from [Mat96, Mat97].

$$P(A|B) = \frac{P(A) \cdot P(B|A)}{P(B)} \tag{3.1}$$

Expanding the probability $P(B)$ for the set of all n possible, mutually exclusive outcomes A we arrive at equation (3.2):

$$P(B) = \sum_{i=1}^{n} P(A_i) \cdot P(B|A_i) \tag{3.2}$$

Combining equations (3.1) and (3.2) we arrive at a generally more useful statement of Bayes's theorem:

$$P(A|B) = \frac{P(A) \cdot P(B|A)}{\sum_{i=1}^{n} P(A_i) \cdot P(B|A_i)} \tag{3.3}$$

The base-rate fallacy is best described through example.[3] Suppose that your doctor performs a test that is 99% accurate, i.e. when the test was administered to a test population all of whom had the disease, 99% of the tests indicated disease, and likewise, when the test population was known to be 100% free of the disease, 99% of the test results were negative. Upon visiting your doctor to learn the results he tells you he has good news and bad news. The bad news is that indeed you tested positive for the disease. The good news however, is that out of the entire population the rate of incidence is only 1/10000, i.e. only 1 in 10000 people have this ailment. What, given this information, is the probability of you having the disease? The reader is encouraged to make a quick "guesstimate" of the answer at this point.

Let us start by naming the different outcomes. Let S denote sick, and $\neg S$, i.e. *not* S, denote healthy. Likewise, let P denote a positive test result and $\neg P$ denote a negative test result. Restating the information above; given: $P(P|S) = 0.99$, $P(\neg P|\neg S) = 0.99$, and $P(S) = 1/10000$, what is the probability $P(S|P)$?

A direct application of equation (3.3) above gives:

$$P(S|P) = \frac{P(S) \cdot P(P|S)}{P(S) \cdot P(P|S) + P(\neg S) \cdot P(P|\neg S)} \tag{3.4}$$

The only probability above which we do not immediately know is $P(P|\neg S)$. This is easily found though, since it is merely $1 - P(\neg P|\neg S) = 1\%$ (likewise, $P(\neg S) = 1 - P(S)$). Substituting the stated values for the different quantities in equation (3.4) gives:

---

[3]This example is from [RN95].

$$P(S|P) = \frac{1/10000 \cdot 0.99}{1/10000 \cdot 0.99 + (1 - 1/10000) \cdot 0.01} = 0.00980\ldots \approx 1\%$$

$$(3.5)$$

That is, that even though the test is 99% certain, your chance of actually having the disease is only $1/100$, because the population of healthy people is much larger than the population with the disease. For a graphical representation, in the form of a Venn diagram, depicting the different outcomes, see Figure 3.1.

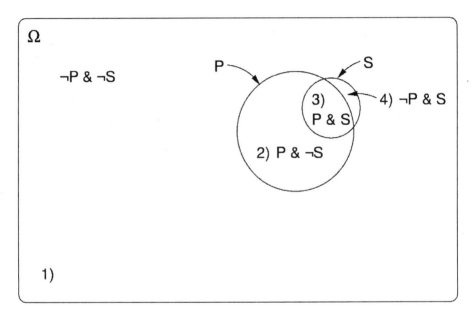

Figure 3.1. Venn diagram of medical diagnostic example

Although the Venn diagram is not to scale it clearly demonstrates the basis of the base-rate fallacy, i.e. that the population in the outcome S is much smaller than that in $\neg S$ and hence, even though $P(P|S) = 99\%$ and $P(\neg P|\neg S) = 99\%$, the relative sizes of the missing 1% in each case—areas 2) and 4) in the diagram—are very different.

Thus when we compare the relative sizes of the four numbered areas in the diagram, and interpret them as probability measures, we can state the desired probability, $P(S|P)$—i.e. "What is the probability that we are in area 3) given that we are inside the P-area?" It may be seen that, area 3) is small relative to the entire P-area, and hence, the fact that the test is positive does not say much, in absolute terms, about our state of health.

This result often surprises people, ourselves included, and the phenomenon—that humans in general do not take the basic rate of incidence, the base-rate, into account when intuitively solving such problems of probability—is aptly named "the base-rate fallacy."

3. The Base-Rate Fallacy in Intrusion Detection

In order to apply this reasoning in computer intrusion detection we must first find, or make reasonable assumptions about the various probabilities.

3.1 Basic Frequency Assumptions

Let us for the sake of further argument hypothesize a figurative computer installation with a few tens of workstations, a few servers—all running UNIX— and a couple of dozen users. Such an installation could produce in the order of 1,000,000 audit records per day with some form of "C2" compliant logging in effect (in itself a testimony to the need for automated intrusion detection).

Suppose further that in such a small installation we would not experience more than a few, say one or two, actual attempted intrusions per day. Even though it is difficult to get any figures for real incidences of attempted computer security intrusions, this does not seem to be an unreasonable number.

Furthermore, assume that at this installation we do not have the manpower to have more than one site security officer—SSO for short—who probably has other duties, and that the SSO, being only human, can only react to a relatively low number of alarms, especially if the false alarm rate is high (50% or so), see Section 3.2.

Even though an intrusion could possibly affect only one audit record, it is likely on average that it will affect a few more than that. Furthermore, a clustering factor actually makes our estimates more conservative, so it was deemed prudent to include one. Using data from a previous study of the trails that SunOS intrusions leave in the system logs [ALGJ98], we can estimate that ten audit records would be affected in the average intrusion.

3.2 Human Machine Interaction in Intrusion Detection

The previous assumptions above are "technical" in nature, i.e. those well versed in the field of computer security can make similar predictions, or adjust the ones above to suit their liking. It is a simple matter to verify or predict similar measures. However, the factor of the performance of the human operator does not lend itself to the same technological estimates. Thus, a crucial question is that of the capacity of the human operator to correctly respond to the output of the system. Especially the operator's capacity to tolerate false alarms.

Unfortunately there have been no experiments concerning these factors in the setting of computer security intrusion detection. There is, however, some research in the context of process automation and plant control, such as would be the case in a (nuclear) power station, paper mill, steel mill, large ship etc.

Broadly speaking, research has shown [Ras86, p. 5] that a human operator (decision maker) in such an environment has to:

Detect the need for intervention and to

observe important data in order to have direction for subsequent activities. He then has to analyze the data in order to

identify the present state of affairs and to

evaluate their possible consequences with reference to operational goals and company policies. Then a

target state into which the system should be transfered has to be chosen, and the

task that the decision maker has to perform is selected from a review of the resources available to reach said target state. When the task has been identified the proper

procedure i.e. how to do it, must be planned and executed.

In our case we have chosen to aid the operator with an intrusion detection system. However we quickly notice the absence of any discussion about the rest of the decision making chain—even though the recovery element has seen some general study—when it comes to the research into human interaction with intrusion detection systems. Most authors don't even discuss the second step in recovery above, namely that of aiding the operator with *observations* about the state of the system. (The normal state of which is most often not known in our case. No-one knows what the traffic on our computer networks typically looks like, hence the reported difficulty of even deciding if something really is amiss [Sto95].)

More specifically, in this particular case, we are interested in the operator's ability to act "correctly" in the presence of false alarms. I.e. how many false alarms an operator can tolerate without loosing his vigilance.

This is a difficult question to answer in this particular context, not only because there has been no research into the question. A few difficulties are:

- First, the modeling of the human operator handling such a highly complex and cognitive task as the detection and resolution of a computer security incident is difficult in general terms. It is doubtful that we will ever reach a quantitative model of human performance and limitations in this area. We can make several qualitative statements however [Wic92, pp. 258].

- Second, several different factors influence the performance of the operator at different times, such as previous experience, level of training, work load, external and internal stresses, state of vigilance etc.

- Third, the human operator is prone to several different kinds of bias when making a decision of this kind, biases relating to his in ability to correctly make statistical estimates, of making correct logical inferences etc. From our perspective the bias of tending to stay with the original hypothesis (that no intrusion has taken place in our case) and not seek disconfirmatory evidence is especially interesting to us [Wic92, pp. 280].

What previous research in other areas seem to tell us specifically about our situation, is that human operators tend to have a very low tolerance for false alarms. During normal operation, humans have a tendency to over trust the infallibility of the automated equipment. However once the equipment is seen to malfunction (raise false alarms in our case) humans tend to mistrust the equipment to a larger degree than what would be warranted by its actual performance. "Trust once betrayed is hard to recover" [Wic92, p. 537] Perhaps surprisingly, there has been little empirical research in this area [Nyg94, Wic92, p. 537].

What studies have been made [Nyg94, Dea72], seem to indicate that our required level of false alarms, 50%, is a *very* conservative estimate. Most human operators will have completely lost faith in the device at that point, opting to treat every alarm with extreme skepticism, if one would be able to speak of a "treatment" at all, the intrusion detection system would most likely be completely ignored in a "civilian" setting.

3.3   Calculation of Bayesian Detection Rates

Let I and $\neg I$ denote *intrusive*, and *non-intrusive* behavior respectively, and A and $\neg A$ denote the presence or absence of an intrusion alarm. We start by naming the four possible cases (false and true positives and negatives) that arise by working backwards from the above set of assumptions:

Detection rate Or *true positive* rate. The probability $P(A|I)$, i.e. that quantity that we can obtain when testing our detector against a set of scenarios we know represent intrusive behavior.

False alarm rate The probability $P(A|\neg I)$, the *false positive* rate, obtained in an analogous manner.

The other two parameters, $P(\neg A|I)$, the *False Negative* rate, and $P(\neg A|\neg I)$, the *True Negative* rate, are easily obtained since they are merely:

$$P(\neg A|I) = 1 - P(A|I); P(\neg A|\neg I) = 1 - P(A|\neg I) \qquad (3.6)$$

Of course, our ultimate interest is that both:

- $P(I|A)$—that an alarm really indicates an intrusion (henceforth called the *Bayesian detection rate* though keeping in line with terminology in other fields, the term *positive predictive value* would perhaps have been a better choice), and

- $P(\neg I|\neg A)$—that the absence of an alarm signifies that we have nothing to worry about,

remain as large as possible.

Applying Bayes's theorem to calculate $P(I|A)$ results in:

$$P(I|A) = \frac{P(I) \cdot P(A|I)}{P(I) \cdot P(A|I) + P(\neg I) \cdot P(A|\neg I)} \qquad (3.7)$$

Likewise for $P(\neg I|\neg A)$:

$$P(\neg I|\neg A) = \frac{P(\neg I) \cdot P(\neg A|\neg I)}{P(\neg I) \cdot P(\neg A|\neg I) + P(I) \cdot P(\neg A|I)} \qquad (3.8)$$

These assumptions give us a value for the rate of incidence of the actual number of intrusions in our system, and its dual (10 audit records per intrusion, 2 intrusions per day, and 1,000,000 audit records per day). Interpreting these as probabilities:

$$P(I) = 1 \left/ \frac{1 \cdot 10^6}{2 \cdot 10} \right. = 2 \cdot 10^{-5};$$
$$P(\neg I) = 1 - P(I) = 0.99998 \qquad (3.9)$$

Inserting equation (3.9) into equation (3.7):

$$P(I|A) = \frac{2 \cdot 10^{-5} \cdot P(A|I)}{2 \cdot 10^{-5} \cdot P(A|I) + 0.99998 \cdot P(A|\neg I)} \qquad (3.10)$$

Studying equation (3.10) we see the base-rate fallacy clearly. By now it should come as no surprise to the reader, since the assumptions made about our system makes it clear that we have an overwhelming number of non-events (benign activity) in our audit trail, and only a few events (intrusions) of any interest. Thus, the factor governing the *detection* rate $(2 \cdot 10^{-5})$ is completely dominated by the factor (0.99998) governing the *false alarm* rate. Furthermore, since $0 \leq P(A|I) \leq 1$, the equation will have its desired maximum for $P(A|I) = 1$ and $P(A|\neg I) = 0$, which results in the most beneficial outcome as far as the *false alarm* rate is concerned. While reaching these values would be an accomplishment indeed, they are hardly attainable in practice. Let us instead plot the value of $P(I|A)$ for a few fixed values of $P(A|I)$ (including

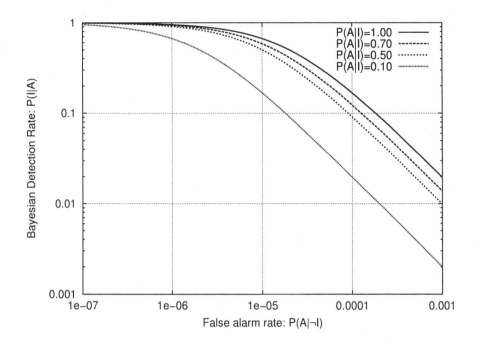

Figure 3.2. Plot of Bayesian detection rate versus false alarm rate

the "best" case $P(A|I) = 1$), as a function of $P(A|\neg I)$ (see Figure 3.2). It should be noted that both axes are logarithmic.

It becomes clear from studying the plot in Figure 3.2 that even for the unrealistically high *detection* rate 1.0 , we have to have a very low *false alarm* rate (on the order of $1 \cdot 10^{-5}$) for the Bayesian detection rate to have a value of 66%, i.e. about two thirds of all alarms will be a true indication of intrusive activity. With a more realistic *detection* rate of, say, 0.7, for the same *false alarm* rate, the value of the Bayesian detection rate is about 58%, nearing fifty-fifty. Even though the number of events (intrusions/alarms) is still low, it is our belief that a low Bayesian detection rate would quickly "teach" the SSO to (un)safely ignore *all* alarms, (especially if the detected intrusions were of a trivial, say probing, nature) even though their absolute numbers would theoretically have allowed a complete investigation of all alarms. This becomes especially true as the system grows; a 50% false alarm rate of in total of 100 alarms would clearly not be tolerable. Note that even quite a large difference in the *detection* rate does not substantially alter the Bayesian detection rate, which instead is dominated by the *false alarm* rate. Whether such a low rate of false alarms is at all attainable is discussed in section 4.

It becomes clear that, for example, a requirement of only 100 false alarms per day is met by a large margin with a *false alarm* rate of $1 \cdot 10^{-5}$. With 10^5 "events" per day, we will see only 1 *false alarm* per day, on average. By the time our ceiling of 100 false alarms per day is met, at a rate of $1 \cdot 10^{-3}$ *false alarms*, even in the best case scenario, our Bayesian detection rate is down to around 2%,[4] by which time no-one will care less when the alarm goes off.

Substituting (3.6) and (3.9) in equation (3.8) gives:

$$P(\neg I | \neg A) = \frac{0.99998 \cdot (1 - P(A|\neg I))}{0.99998 \cdot (1 - P(A|\neg I)) + 2 \cdot 10^{-5} \cdot (1 - P(A|I))} \quad (3.11)$$

A quick glance at the resulting equation (3.11) raises no cause for concern. The large $P(\neg I)$ factor (0.99998) will completely dominate the result, giving it values near 1.0 for the values of $P(A|\neg I)$ under discussion here, regardless of the value of $P(A|I)$.

This is the base-rate fallacy in reverse, if you will, since we have already demonstrated that the problem is that we will set off the alarm too many times in response to non-intrusions, combined with the fact that we do not have many intrusions to begin with. Truly a question of finding a needle in a haystack.

The author does not see how the situation underlying the base-rate fallacy problem will change for the better in years to come. On the contrary, as computers get faster they will produce more audit data, while it is doubtful that intrusive activity will increase at the same rate. In fact, it would have to increase at a substantially higher rate for it to have any effect on the previous calculations, and were it ever to reach levels sufficient to have such an effect—say 30% or more—the installation would no doubt have a serious problem on its hands, to say the least! It would most definitely not have a *detection* problem anymore.

4.   Impact on Intrusion Detection Systems

As stated in the introduction to this book, approaches to intrusion detection can be divided into three major groups, *signature*-based, *anomaly*-based, and *combined detectors*, i.e. detectors that operate with a model of both benign and malicious behavior. The previous section developed requirements regarding *false alarm* rates and *detection* rates in intrusion detection systems in order to make them useful in the stated scenario. This section will compare these requirements with reported results on the effectiveness of intrusion detection systems.

It can be argued that this reasoning does not apply to anomaly-based intrusion detection. In some cases anomaly-based detection tries not to detect

---

[4]Another way of calculating that differs from equation (3.10) is of course to realise that 100 false alarms and only a maximum of 2 possible valid alarms gives: $\frac{2}{2+100} \approx 2\%$.

intrusions per se, but rather to differentiate between two different subjects, flagging anomalous behavior in the hopes that it is indicative of a stolen user identity for instance, see for example [LB98], which even though it reports performance figures, is not directly applicable here. However, we think the previous scenario is useful as a description of a wide range of more "immediate," often network-based, attacks, where we will not have had the opportunity to observe the intruder for an extended period of time "prior" to the attack.

4.1   ROC Curve Analysis

There are general results in detection and estimation theory that state that the *detection* and *false alarm* rates are linked [Tre68], though the extent to which they are applicable here is still an open question. Obviously, if the *detection* rate is 1, saying that all events are intrusions, we will have a *false alarm* rate of 1 as well, and conversely the same can be said for the case where the rates are 0.[5] Intuitively, we see that by classifying more and more events as intrusive—in effect relaxing our requirements on what constitutes an intrusion—we will increase our *detection* rate, but also misclassify more of the benign activity, and hence increase our *false alarm* rate.

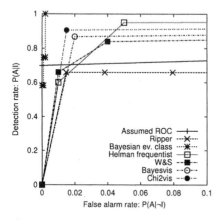 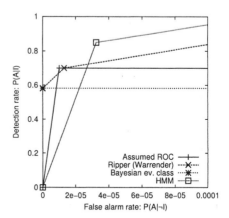

Figure 3.3. ROC-curves for the "low performers"

Figure 3.4. ROC-curve for the "high performers"

---

[5]If you call everything with a large red nose a clown, you'll spot all the clowns, but also Santa's reindeer, Rudolph, and vice versa.

Plotting the *detection* rate as a function of the *false alarm* rate we end up with what is called a ROC—Receiver Operating Characteristic—curve. (For a general introduction to ROC curves, and detection and estimation theory, see [Tre68].) We have already stated that the points $(0;0)$ and $(1;1)$ are members of the ROC curve for any intrusion detector. Furthermore, the curve between these points is convex; were it concave, we would do better to reverse our decision. Nor can it contain any dips, as that would in effect indicate a faulty, non-optimal detector, since a randomized test would then be better; we could achieve a detector operating at any point along the interpolated line between the two points straddling the dip, by making a weighted randomized decision involving the detectors at the straddling points. If we wanted a detector with a performance corresponding to the point half way between the two straddling points we would just need to toss a fair coin and run the lower detector when the coin came up *heads* and the upper when the coin came up *tails*. We're not seriously suggesting that anyone actually build such a detector, but the observation serves as a check against poorly performing detectors. If your detector ROC has a dip, you should be able to do better in that region of the curve. See "Assumed ROC" curve in figures 3.3 and 3.4 for the ROC curve that depicts our previous example.

We see that the required ROC curve has a very sharp rise from $(0;0)$ since we quickly have to reach acceptable *detection* rate values (0.7) while still keeping the *false alarm* rate under control.

4.2   Previous Experimental Intrusion Detection Evaluations

When we first wrote this paper, the literature was not overladen with experimental results from tests of intrusion detection systems. Now, some five years later, this is still very much the case, even though quite a few extra results have been reported. Ideally we would like several different results from the different classes of intrusion detectors, evaluated on the same data sets. Unfortunately there only exists a few reports of anomaly detection performance in this regard e.g [HL93] with no example of specification based intrusion detection, and one independent report of a classical detector [WFP99]. Several signature based detectors have been tested for DARPA by however [GLC+98].

Unfortunately data from the evaluation performed by DARPA by Lincoln Labs at MIT [LGG+98, GLC+98] is unavailable to us for independent evaluation because of U.S. export restrictions, and furthermore serious doubts as to the quality of parts of that data have been raised [MC03]; it turns out that some of the fields in the network data differ between the simulated background traffic and the injected attacks in a manner that makes them completely trivial to differentiate! Furthermore this difference has no bearing on the attack versus benign traffic dichotomy whatsoever, but is purely an artifact of the merging process. It is currently unknown to what degree the evaluation of the intrusion detectors studied below suffered from this flaw, i.e. to what extent they picked up on the fields that differed, or whether they operated without specific knowledge of this difference. It should be noted that this flaw is asymmetric in that, if the detector takes advantage of it, it will tend to make the detector look better than it should. It will never make detectors look worse. Other criticisms of the DARPA evaluation have also been raised [McH00].

When this paper was first written, the details of this study had not been published, but since then a paper [LFG+00] and a very detailed report of the data and procedures of the experiment have been made available [HLF+01]. Thus, what has been made known about the DARPA evaluation is that the study was conducted using a simulated network of workstations, transmitting simulated traffic. This traffic was generated based on real traffic observed on a large US Air Force base, and a large research institute. This of course lends some credibility to an argument about the generality of the background traffic. Of course, the degree to which the background traffic is representative of the background traffic in the field is a crucial question when it comes to the value of the test as an indicator of false alarm rates during normal usage.

In the test, a number of different attacks were then inserted into the simulated network, including denial of service attacks against the network, and "root" exploits against individual workstations. The experimenters invited several different intrusion detectors to participate in the study. These were all signature based detectors operating on either network or host data. Even though there is more going on behind the scenes (the detection rate varies between approximately 20%–90% for the best scoring detector for all attacks) we will limit the presentation the best overall scores for the conglomerate of detectors in the network study, i.e. the detector resulting from combining the four different detectors and choosing the best performer in all instances. Note that this may not be realistic, since it would be difficult to perform this conglomeration in practice, to say the least.

Also not all detectors performed equally well when dealing with all intrusions, and it is a general criticism that in the case of signature based detection, the designer of the signature can easily trade off detection rate for false alarm rate by varying the generality of the signature. The more general it is, the more variations of the same intrusive behavior it will detect, but at the cost of a higher false alarm rate. It is not known to what extent the DARPA evaluation used variations of the attacks presented to the designers of the intrusion detection systems for training purposes, in the final evaluation. This is an important point in that when such systems are commercialized, it will be impossible to keep the detection signatures secret from the would be intruders, and the more savvy among them will of course attempt to vary their techniques in order to evade detection. A recent paper investigates just how brittle such signatures can be in the face of modification for the purpose of evasion of the IDS [VRB04].

Much more can be said about this evaluation, but we will limit our comments to the above. Of course choosing the best performer makes our comparison more conservative, even though this is somewhat moderated by the flaws inherent in the data.

The second study [WFP99] lists test results for six different intrusion detection methods that have been applied to traces of system calls made into the operating system kernel by nine different privileged applications in a UNIX environment. Most of these traces were obtained from "live" data sources, i.e. the systems from which they were collected were production systems. The authors' hypothesis is that short sequences of system calls exhibit patterns that describe normal, benign activity, and that different intrusion detection mechanisms can be trained to detect abnormal patterns, and flag these as intrusive. The researchers thus trained the intrusion detection systems using part of the "normal" traffic, and tested their false alarm rate on the remaining "normal" traffic. They then trained the systems on intrusive scenarios, and inserted such intrusions into normal traffic to ascertain the detection rate. The experimental method is thus close to the one described in Sections 2 and 3 of this chapter. This study evaluated as one of the systems the self learning "classical" detector, RIPPER, described by Lee [Lee99].

The third study [HL93] is a treatise on the fundamental limits of the effectiveness of intrusion detection. The authors constructs a model of the intrusive and normal process and investigate the properties of this model from an anomaly intrusion detection perspective under certain assumptions. Their approach differs from ours in that they do not provide any estimates of the parameters in their model, opting instead to explore the limits of effectiveness when such information is unavailable. Of greatest interest here is their conclusion in which the authors plot experimental data for two implementations, one a frequentist detector that—it is claimed—is close to optimal under the given circumstances, and an earlier tool designed by the authors, Wisdom & Sense [VL89]. Unfortunately, only one type of anomaly detection system, one that operates with descriptive statistics of the behavior of the subject, is covered. As previously mentioned, specification based intrusion detection is not covered, and furthermore, neither are more "sophisticated" detectors, such as neural network based detectors (such as [DBS92]), that take time series behavior of the subject into account.

The fourth study is from a more recent attempt at optimizing the combination of several smaller (i.e. reduced in scope) anomaly detectors using Bayesian belief networks applied to traces of system calls [KMRV03]. The resulting detector was trained and applied to the system call traces of a few different server processes that were exploited as a result of network based (or network launched) attacks in the Lincoln Labs evaluation. As the detector didn't see the network traffic directly it did not suffer from the flaw in network data described earlier.

The results from the studies above and from our own two visualizing detectors (named *Bayesvis* and *Chi2vis*) described later in this book, have been plotted in figures 3.3 and 3.4. Where a range of values were given in the original presentation, the best—most "flattering" if you will—value was chosen. Furthermore, since not all the work cited to provided actual numerical data, some points are based on our interpretation of the presented values. In the case of the DARPA study the results were rescaled to conform with our requirements. (The original DARPA test assumes 66,000 events per day instead of our 100,000 events per day.) We feel that these are accurate enough for the purpose of giving the reader an idea of the performance of the systems.

The cited work can be roughly divided into two classes depending on the minimum false alarm rate values that are presented, and hence, for clarity, the presentation has been divided into figures, where the first (Figure 3.3) presents the first class, with larger values for the false alarm rate. These consists of most of the anomaly detection results in this study with the exception of the more modern detector reported in [KMRV03] named *Bayesian ev. class* in the figure. In the figure "Helman frequentist," and "W&S" denote the detection results from [HL93]. It is interesting to note, especially in the light of the strong claims made by the authors of this evaluation, that all of the presented false alarm rates are several orders of magnitude larger than the requirements put forth in Section 3 and that a later anomaly detection systems surpasses it. It should be noted that the detectors developed by the authors were run on web server data that contained only the *types* of attacks and not the instances such as for all other detector results reported here. Hence if easily detected types of attack were very prevalent in the data this would tend to underplay the performance of these detectors, and vice versa. They are included here mainly to illustrate the fact that even though they report false alarm rates that are much higher than those postulated here, they still work (or so we would claim) in that they address another facet of the problem, namely that of how to present the data to the operator in such a way as to make the false alarms (and true alarms for that matter) as easily identifiable as possible, permitting the operator to remain effective.

The second class of detectors, depicted in Figure 3.4, consists of the average results of Ripper [Lee99], a high performance Hidden Markov Model detector (labeled "HMM" in the figure) tested by Warrander et. al. in [WFP99], and the DARPA results. Here the picture is less clear. The authors report false alarm results close to zero for lower detection rates, with one performance point nearly overlapping our required performance point. The HMM detector is also close to what we would require. It is more difficult to generalize these results, since they are based on one method of data selection, and the authors do not make as strong a claim as those made for the previous set of detectors. The DARPA data from [GLC$^+$98], show up as "DARPA TCP" in Figure 3.4. They are also in the vicinity of the required performance point, but the question of the generality of the training/test data, and hence the results, remains. Note that the more modern anomaly detection system (Bayes ev. class) is plotted here also because it has one operational point at a detection rate of just under 0.6 for a false alarm rate of *zero*. It is also interesting to note (though difficult to see in the figures) that it holds this constant detection rate for false alarm rate increasing to close to 0.001. This phenomenon repeats itself for the following steps up in detection rate, where the same detection rate is reported for a range of false alarm rates, giving the ROC curve a stair-like appearance. As we have discussed previously, this means that there is, in theory at least, room for improvement, as a simple randomized weighing of these points would lead to a curve consisting of a convex polygon shape. So even though this detector does not reach our goal for detection rate, it is of course a strong result in that it manages a decent detection rate at zero false alarms despite being a pure anomaly detector.

5. Future Directions

One sticking point is the basic probabilities that the previous calculations are based on. These probabilities are subjective at present, but future work should include measurement either to attempt to calculate these probabilities from observed frequencies—the *frequentist* approach—or to deduce these probabilities from some model of the intrusive process and the intrusion detection system— the *objectivist* approach. The latter would in turn require real world observation to formulate realistic parameters for the models.

Furthermore, this discourse treats the intrusion detection problem as a binary decision problem, i.e. that of deciding whether there has been an "intrusion" or not. The work presented does not differentiate between the different kinds of intrusions that can take place, and nor does it recognize that different types of intrusions are not equally difficult or easy to detect. Thus on a more detailed level, the intrusion detection problem is not a binary but rather an n-valued problem.

Another area that needs attention is that of the SSO's capabilities. How does the human-computer interaction take place, and precisely which Bayesian detection rates would an SSO tolerate under what circumstances for example? This is the question that we address in the remainder of the book.

6. Further Reading

Since the first publication of the material on which this chapter is based, others have approached the problem of determining the effectiveness of intrusion detection, most notably Lee et. al. [LFM$^+$02] where they expand on the model presented here by considering different types of attacks and adding varying costs for their detection and failure of detection.

7. Conclusions

This chapter demonstrated that intrusion detection in a realistic setting is harder than was perhaps thought. This is due to the base-rate fallacy problem, because of which the factor limiting the performance of an intrusion detection system is not the ability to identify behavior correctly as intrusive, but rather *its ability to suppress false alarms*. A very high standard, less than $1/100,000$ per "event" given the stated set of circumstances, will have to be reached for the intrusion detection system to live up to these expectations as far as *effectiveness* is concerned.

The cited studies of intrusion detector performance that were plotted and compared indicate that anomaly-based methods may have had a long way to go before they could reach these standards, since their false alarm rates were several orders of magnitude larger than what we demand, but that more recent results showed reason for hope in this respect. When we come to the case of signature-based detection methods the picture was less clear. Even though the cited work seems to indicate that current signature intrusion detectors can operate close to the required performance point, how well these results generalize in the field was and is still an open question. We only have three data point when it comes to the more qualified "classical" detectors, and the first seemed to perform on par with signature based detectors while our own approaches were several orders of magnitude off.

Chapter 4

VISUALIZING INTRUSIONS: WATCHING THE WEBSERVER

As we learned in the previous chapter, a significant problem with intrusion detection systems is the high number of false alarms. In this chapter[1] we begin our investigation into the use of *information visualization* [CMS99, Spe01] in intrusion detection. The main problem with applying information visualization to intrusion detection is the large amount of data that the user is faced with. To address this we apply an anomaly detection inspired method to reduce the log to manageable proportions, before applying graph visualization to understand the actual data. The hypothesis is that this enables the user to benefit from the strengths of both visualization—quickly making sense of medium size data sets, and anomaly detection—summarily discarding large amounts of uninteresting data, all the while avoiding the problems of visualization having a limit to the amount of data that can reasonably be handled, and anomaly detection having a high false alarm rate for decent detection rates.

We believe that the application of visualization to intrusion detection has a number of other desirable effects; mainly that the site does not need as detailed a security policy as with pre-programmed intrusion detection systems, and that an understanding of the underlying security principles being violated is furthered. Applying information visualization to the problem of intrusion detection may seem obvious (at least in retrospect) but success is by no means assured. The main problem is one of scale: most information visualization techniques cannot be used to visualize the large amounts of data with which we are faced, at least not in a straightforward manner. On the order of thousands of data objects are the norm, rather than the hundreds of thousands we are faced with here [Spe01].

---

[1]This chapter is based on [Axe04b].

Therefore we investigate the use of some form of anomaly based log reduction to reduce these logs prior to visualization, drawing on the strengths of both methods, to combat their respective weaknesses.

To that end we have chosen to perform an empirical study of the access requests made to a fairly large public webserver. We develop and apply an anomaly based log reduction system to the access requests to reduce their number to manageable size. The hypothesis being that we can tolerate a high number of false alarms since we will visualize the output. Thus a simple anomaly based scheme will suffice. We then develop a visualization technique that visualizes the structure of the selected access requests, and apply the technique to the reduced log to identify benign and malicious accesses. The chapter ends with a more detailed study of the results of the visualization technique and the log reduction system.

1.   The Experimental System

For the experiment, a webserver access log was studied. HTTP is of course a major protocol (indeed to the general public the World Wide Web *is* the Internet), and very important from a business perspective in many installations. Also we believe that there would be security relevant activity to be found in the webserver log under study, since there have been numerous (mostly automated) attacks reported e.g. [CER01b, CER01a]. In addition, webserver logs are an example of application level logging which is an area that has received relatively little attention. Attention instead being focused on lower level network protocols or lower level host based logs. Also important is the fact that webserver logs are less sensitive from a privacy perspective—something that is not true when monitoring network traffic in general—since it is a service we provide to the general public who have lower expectation of privacy, and hence act accordingly. We recognize that this may not be true of every webserver in operation.

It should be stressed that the primary interest is in experimenting with the effectiveness of the combination of visualization and anomaly based log reduction, *not* in producing a realistic tool for usage in the field. Unfortunately there is a dearth of publicly available corpora useful for intrusion detection research. The most popular such corpora is the Lincoln Labs DARPA evaluation data, even though it is not without its flaws [McH00]. As it is export controlled it is unfortunately unavailable to us.

The webserver under study serves a university Computer Science department. The server was running Apache version 1.3.26, and set to log according to the *common* log format. The log consists of a line based text file with each line representing a single HTTP access request. The *request* field i.e. the actual HTTP request sent to the server, is important as it is the central point of many attacks against a web server. The request field consists of the request method ("GET", "HEAD", "CONNECT", etc), followed by the *path* to the resource the client is requesting, and the method of access (e.g. "HTTP 1.1"). The *path* in turn can be divided into components separated by certain reserved characters.

We studied the log for the month of November 2002, since it was believed that it would contain security relevant incidents, and we had access to later logs with which to compare the results. The access log contained ca. 1.2 million records. Selecting the actual request fields and removing duplicates ca. 220000 unique requests were identified. Because of their importance it is these unique requests that will be studied in the rest of the chapter.

2. The Log Reduction Scheme

The log reduction scheme is based on descriptive statistics; in this case the frequencies with which events occur. This is in the same vein as seminal intrusion detection systems such as NIDES [AFV95], though the approach here is simpler still. In order to classify the requests according to how unusual they are they are first cut up into components letting the reserved characters " ?:&=+$," separate the fields. For example a request such as "GET /pub/index.html HTTP 1.1", is separated into the components "GET", "pub","index.html", "HTTP" and "1.1". The absolute frequencies of the fields as they appear in different unique request strings are counted.

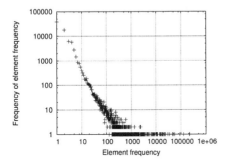 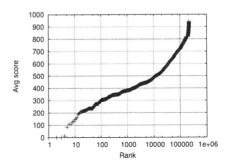

Figure 4.1. Frequencies of component frequencies

Figure 4.2. Requests sorted by lowest score

The request as a whole is scored by calculating the average of the absolute frequencies of the path components and hence requests consisting of unusual components have a low score, signifying that they are viewed as *anomalous*. However, studying the *frequencies* of the *component frequencies* we see that a few high scoring elements (such as "GET") could skew (i.e. drive up) the average. Therefore a *cutoff* is applied. Figure 4.1 lists the frequencies of the frequencies of the components. Studying the figure we see that a cutoff of 1000 seems reasonable since most of the activity appears to have died off by then.

There are very few components with frequencies above 1000 and since they represent elements that are very common, they would tend to drown the lower frequency components we are interested in. Figure 4.2 plots the scores of the requests as a function of the ordering. The lowest scoring 5200 accesses are selected since that gives us a manageable amount of data to visualize.

3. Visualizing the Lowest Scoring Requests

The idea is to visualize the structure (and clusterings) of the various requests, the hypothesis being that differences in structure will enable the user to (relatively) quickly identify patterns of benign and malicious access. To accomplish this, the requests are cut into components as described in the previous section. The resulting components are visualized as a general graph where adjacent components in the request string are linked via directed edges in the graph. Using the same example as before: the request "GET /pub/index.html HTTP 1.1", is cut up into nodes ("GET" etc.) with directed edges connecting "GET" with "pub", "pub" with "index.html" etc.

To visualize the resulting graph the graph visualization tool *Tulip* was chosen.[2] Tulip has extensive features for interactive viewing and manipulation of general graphs. These aspects are unfortunately difficult to capture in writing (even with illustrations).

To perform the actual detection the 5200 lowest scoring accesses is visualized in Figure 4.3 [3] as a three dimensional general graph. The circular structure at the top of the graph that can be seen to reach almost all of the rest of the graph is the "GET"-node. Note that the edges are not drawn as solid lines, since this would completely occlude the view.

At first Figure 4.3 may look daunting, but closer scrutiny reveals several large features. Close to the center of the picture for example, we see a large double ring structure. Contrasting it with all other features, it looks rather unique, there is no other structure that looks similar (at least on this level), so we decide to investigate further.

Enlarging the feature in question leads to Figure 4.4. Following the links (which is somewhat difficult to do in the static display here) we learn of a loose structure that starts with either "cgi-bin" or "cgi-local" and progresses via "recipient", "subject" and then the unlikely looking random text strings. It turns out that these text strings are in fact recipient email addresses for *aol.com* and *hotmail.com* email users. The message to be mailed in many cases (but not all) purports to be from John Doe, and is simply "Is anybody out there?" So this particular access pattern seems to be a *spam attack*, trying to use a misconfigured HTML to mail gateway that is commonly available. It was

---

[2]Tulip is freely available under the GPL from "http://www.tulip-software.org".
[3]The PDF-rendition of this graph may be clearer than a printed image.

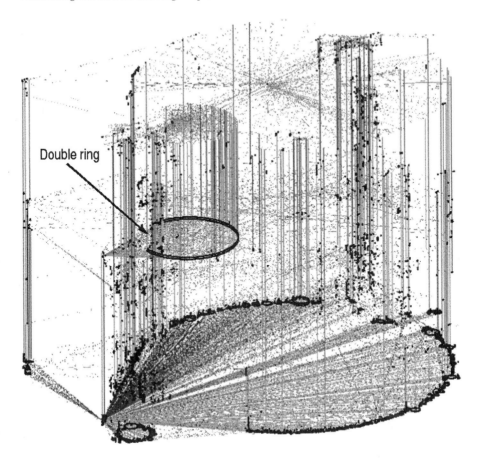

Figure 4.3. Graph of the lowest scoring requests

not active on the server however. The unlikely looking recipient names are probably automatically generated and the messages sent in the hope of eliciting a response and in doing so finding legitimate email addresses. Note that a tree visualization would have been less powerful here, since there are two major (early in the request) parents of this particular pattern: "cgi-bin" and "cgi-local". When visualized as a tree these branches would not have shared the latter features, even when they would have been the same.

We are usually not so fortunate as to be able to identify attacks the moment we lay our eyes on the graph. Instead we have to repeat the above detailed analysis. It so happens that all the other major features that are identifiable in Figure 4.3 are uninteresting. However, they are all also much more regular than the pattern we have just seen. This makes it possible for the user to eliminate many edges by eliminating fewer key parent nodes, slashing away what amounts

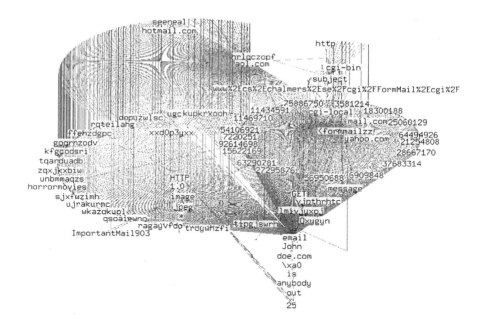

Figure 4.4. Zoom on feature (Spam attack in this case)

to whole (improper) subtrees, and this fairly large graph can be whittled down with a relatively modest amount of effort.[4]

An example of this process is depicted in Figure 4.5.[5] The accesses to files belonging to the user *carlsson* form a regular subtree that is easily identified as having nothing of a security relevant nature and hence easily discarded. This subgraph contains the data from 145 access requests, letting us discard some 3% of the reduced log in one fell swoop. Looking at the distribution of accesses in similar subgraphs, the twenty largest benign subgraphs (ranging from 213 to 59 access requests respectively) contain 42% of the access requests under scrutiny, and the first 180 benign subgraphs contain some 80% of all access requests in the reduced log. Hence most benign requests can be easily discarded.

A further illustration of this process can be seen in Figure 4.6. This also shows how a benign subgraph can appear when it has not been isolated (as in Figure 4.5). As we can see in this example it is still not too difficult to make sense of the access requests that form this graph (nor indeed to realize that

---

[4]It should be noted that Tulip is not the *perfect* tool in this respect. After a while it becomes cost effective to eliminate the requests from the input data itself and restarting Tulip. In our experiment the elimination was performed by judicious use of the UNIX tools *sort*, *grep* etc.

[5]For the purpose of illustration the corresponding access requests here have been isolated to make the graph clearer.

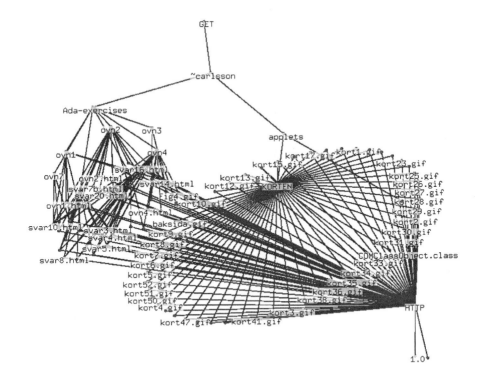

Figure 4.5. Zoom on feature (benign accesses forming a subgraph, isolated)

they're all benign). For the graph in Figure 4.6: 52 access request begin with "02", 49 with "02/infovis", 33 with "02/infovis/literature" (and incidentally the "02/ubicomp" branch only contains 3 distinct access requests). Thus this graph contains about a third as many benign access requests as the graph in Figure 4.5. Unfortunately not all subgraphs that are visible in Figure 4.3 are of this type. As an example Figure 4.7 contains a graph that isn't very easy to make sense of and eliminate as benign off hand. In this case it turns out that it is indeed benign, but more work has to be expended to arrive at that conclusion. The situation is helped somewhat by leaving the troublesome subgraphs for the latter stages of the analysis, when most of the simple benign subgraphs have been eliminated as this improves layout and reduces occlusion.

After about one to two hours we arrive at the distilled requests that we cannot eliminate as benign. Since user experiments are yet to be performed on this method, a more precise time estimate cannot be given with any certainty. These requests will be discussed in more detail in section 4.

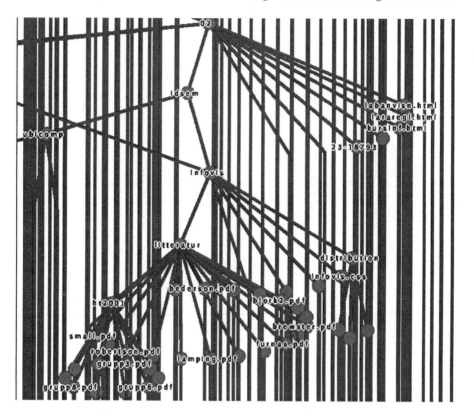

Figure 4.6. Zoom on feature (benign accesses forming a subgraph, in vivo)

4.   Detailed Analysis of the Features Found

The remaining accesses were classified into two categories, *suspect* and *intrusive*. The reason for using a *suspect* class is that since this is data from the field and the intentions of the entity submitting the request are not known, it is sometimes difficult to decide whether a request is the result of an intrusive process, the result of a flaw in the software that submitted it or a mistake by its user. Also, some accesses are just plain peculiar (for want of a better word), and even though they are probably benign, they serve no obvious purpose. As the *suspect* class, consists of accesses that we don't mind if they are brought to the attention of the operator, but on the other hand, as they are not proper indications of intrusions, we will not include them in the experiment.

The *intrusive* class was further subdivided into seven different subclasses that correspond to metaclasses (i.e. each of these metaclasses consists of several types of attacks, each of which may be a part of one or several *instances* of attacks) of the attacks that were observed:

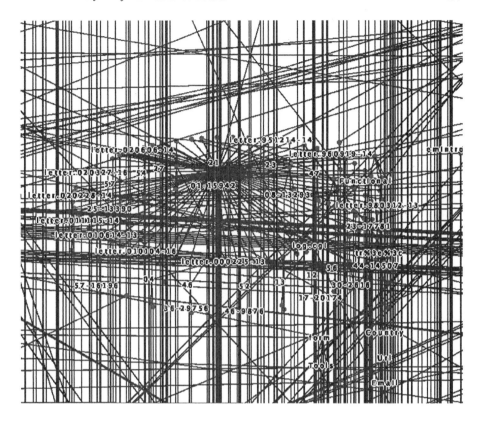

Figure 4.7. Zoom on feature (benign accesses forming a not very clear subgraph)

Formmail attacks The department was subjected to a spam attack, where spammers tried to exploit a commonly available web mail form to send unsolicited mail via our server. This type of attack stood out, with many different requests found.

Unicode attacks These are attacks against the Microsoft IIE web server, where the attacker tries to gain access to shells and scripts by providing a path argument that steps backward (up) in the file tree and then down into a system directory by escaping the offending "\..\" sequence in various ways.[6] IIS protects against this attack by first checking the URL for the "\..\" character sequence, or repetitions thereof, and disallowing the access if found. However, it is possible to trick IIS into allowing such sequences by escaping the offending backslash character, and send an URL that contains e.g.

---

[6]See e.g. "http://builder.com.com/5100-6387_14-1044883-2.html".

"\..%255C..\". IIS will not consider this URL "dangerous" since it does not explicitly contain the parent directory character sequence. However, IIS will then proceed to interpret the escape sequence in two steps (in violation of the HTTP RFC) as consisting of first "\..%5C..\" and then finally as "\..\..\" since the hexadecimal representation of the ASCII codes for "%" and "\" are *0x25* and *0x5C* respectively. Many variations on this scheme are present in the log data.

Proxy attacks The attacker tried to access other resources on the Internet, such as web servers or IRC servers *via* our web server, hoping that it would be misconfigured to proxy such requests. We suppose that this is an attempt to either circumvent restrictive firewalls, or more likely, to disguise the origin of the original request, making tracking and identification more difficult.

Pathaccess attacks These are more direct attempts to access command interpreters, cgi scripts or sensitive system files such as password files. A major subclass here is trying to access back doors known to be left behind by other successful system penetrations (by worms for example). Also configuration files of web applications (e.g. web store software) was targeted. Attempts to gain access to the configuration files of the webserver itself were also spotted. These attacks are all different from the *Unicode attacks* above in that no attempt at obscuring the access request was made. These attacks rely instead on the web server being installed (or previously subverted) to incorrectly provide access to these resources.

Cgi-bin attacks Attacks against cgi scripts that are commonly available on web sites and may contain security flaws. We believe the availability of several cgi script security testing tools to be the reason for the variety of cgi probes present in our data. Although the the formmail script probed for above is technically a cgi-bin attack, those invocations of the script that tried to send email as a probing attack (evident from the *subject* and *recipient* fields) were classified as a *formmail* attack and those that only probed for the presence of the formmail script were classified as a cgi-bin attack.

Buffer overrun Only a few types of buffer overruns were found in our log data. All of these are known to be indicative of worms targeting the Microsoft IIS web server. They are easily identifiable from the prefix of the path, their length and from the fact that they contain long runs of the same character ("A" or "N" respectively).

Misc This class contains seven accesses we are fairly certain are malicious in nature, but which don't fit in any of the previous classes. They are various probes using the *OPTIONS* request method, and a mixture of *GET* and *POST* requests that target the root of the file system. Searching available sources it has been impossible to find any description of exactly which weaknesses these requests target.

The *intrusive* class (minus the *formmail* attack in Figure 4.4) is depicted in a two dimensional flat graph in Figure 4.8 and the three dimensional graphs we are accustomed to in Figure 4.9. We directly see a few security relevant features (i.e. features that stand apart from benign accesses). One such feature is the "system32"/"command.exe" tail in the lower middle of Figure 4.8. This tail is common to many different branches from one of the roots of the graph and turns out to be a strong indicator of the *unicode* attack discussed above. Another peculiar cluster is at the top, second from the left, and it turns out to be instances of the meta class *proxy attacks*.

As we can see from the graphs there are many variations on the basic IIS encoding attack being tried against the server, although the graph of course does not list the actual attacks themselves. It would be interesting to study to what extent the graph predicts (all/most) possible attacks (i.e. by following one branch from the root to a leaf, do we get an executable attack that is not present in the log file proper). The overflow attacks are simple buffer overruns against fixed length buffers without adequate overflow protection, in our case these take the form of very long components (formed of a string beginning with repetitions of the character "N" or "A") followed by escaped shell code. Searching security sources we find that the first of these is characteristic of the Code Red worm.

We will discuss the structure of these attacks in section 6, but for now it will suffice to note that the attacks often come with a *tail* attached. The reason seems to be that attacks that show some diversity nevertheless share common features that may come at any position in the request, while this is not true for normal accesses. In the case of unicode attacks we see it is the "payload" i.e. the commands that the attacker wishes to execute that show many similarities, greater similarities in fact than the encoded path that leads to it However, despite this structure apparent in the attacks, comparing e.g. Figure 4.5 to Figure 4.8 indicates that the visualization method is better suited to *eliminate* benign requests than to *detect* malicious requests. Which is just as well given that there are many more benign requests than malicious ones; and in fact the *false alarms* suppression capability of an intrusion detection system determines its effectiveness [Axe00a].

5. Effectiveness of the Log Reduction Scheme

In order to evaluate the effectiveness of the log reduction scheme we analyzed the entire 220000 unique web requests by hand.

The access requests were classified into the three categories: *normal*, *intrusive* and *suspect* as before. Furthermore the *intrusive* class was divided into the seven subclasses discussed earlier. This further subdivision benefits the in-

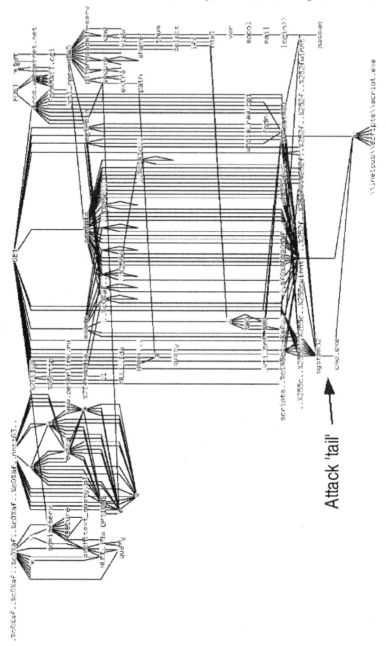

Figure 4.8. The remaining accesses deemed to be intrusion attempts, 2D graph

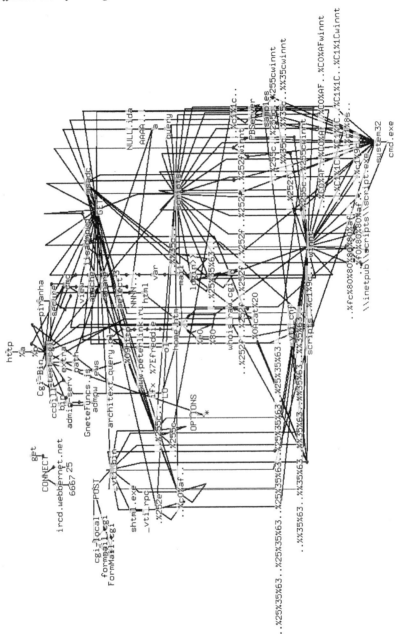

Figure 4.9. The remaining accesses deemed to be intrusion attempts, 3D graph

vestigation of the effectiveness of the log reduction mechanism since it avoids reporting results that might indicate an overall satisfactory detection rate, but on closer study turn out to be lacking in detection capability in any of the seven areas.[7] A summary of how many of the different classes of attacks the log reduction mechanism detected can be found in table 4.1.

Instances of the class *suspect* are not considered false alarms when they occur in the output of the log reduction tool, but on the other hand will not be considered missed attacks when they do not.

Attack	Total	Alarms	Detection rate (%)
Formmail	285	282	99
Unicode	79	79	100
Proxy	9	5	56
Pathaccess	71	16	23
Cgi-bin	219	17	8
Buffer overrun	3	2	66
Miscellaneous	7	2	29
All attacks	673	403	60

Table 4.1. Detection rates of the log reduction mechanism

As we can see in table 4.1, the log reduction mechanism faired well, it managed to preserve evidence of all seven classes of attacks in the reduced log. In light of these results we would not hesitate to claim the log reduction mechanism a success from the point of view of detection rate, even though it did not do spectacularly well in all classes, especially in the classes that were most similar to normal traffic, which is only to be expected.

The discussion of false alarm rates is complicated by the fact that anomaly detection is not actually done, but log reduction. The difference is that an anomaly detection system reports on the *absolute* abnormality of a request, while the log reduction system reports on the *relative* abnormality of a request. The corresponding anomaly detection system would produce a variable number of alarms indicating the level of intrusive activity, but the log reduction scheme will always report the same number of "alarms" regardless, as a suitable number of "alarms" are selected to perform visualization on. Thus the notion of *false alarm rate* is not well defined in this context (see Chapter 4).

Table 4.2 below lists the absolute values of the number of *attacks, normal traffic* and *suspect traffic* that are evident in the whole data set and in the reduced log. As might have been expected the number of benign accesses in the reduced

[7]This might well have been the case since the distribution of different accesses in each of the seven subclasses turns out to be highly skewed and so doing well in one class would skew the overall result.

log is quite high. Circa 86% of the reduced log contains benign traffic. (Note that this number would not correspond to the *false alarm rate*, but rather the *Bayesian false alarm rate* as defined in Chapter 4. The true false alarm rate would be even higher.) This is acceptable since the number of accesses are kept within reasonable limits for the chosen visualization method and the log reduction mechanism has a sufficiently high detection rate.

Access type	All accesses	Alarms
Attacks	673	403
Normal traffic	215504	4499
Suspect	115	28
Total	220000	5200

Table 4.2. Summary of the true and false alarms of the log reduction mechanism

Note that it is pointless to compare the results from the system presented here with that of popular signature based systems such as *Snort* [Roe99], since these rely on previous external knowledge of intrusions. There is unfortunately a dearth of suitable publicly available anomaly detection systems with which to compare the results, though that would be more useful.

6. Discussion

How does the present method compare with spending the same amount of time going through a false alarm list from an intrusion detection system? This is of course difficult to answer, but one could argue that with the visualization approach the user has spent time actually learning about the type of traffic the webserver sees, knowledge that can be used to make the site run better/smoother. This is not generally the case when watching the output of an intrusion detection system.

This generalized knowledge—patterns that are distinct from benign traffic have been found, no benign traffic contains the kind of encoding that the encoding attacks does—can of course be used to program a signature based intrusion detection system. We conjecture this approach would work well, since site-specific knowledge helps to identify what parts of these intrusions that are unique to attacks and do not occur in normal traffic to that site. When performing intrusion detection the best results are achieved when there is a model of both the normal and the intrusive traffic [LX01]. At the very least this knowledge can be used when tuning a signature based intrusion detection system, something which is always necessary.

The anomaly based log reduction system faired well, and it is believed that it would furthermore be difficult to try to circumvent it by injecting similar fields in other fake access requests to try and drive up the frequencies of the interesting fields. This is because such accesses would by their very nature not be successful either as attacks, or as access requests. Taking the result code (i.e. 404) into account when performing the log reduction would eliminate these fake accesses. This would perhaps come at the cost of a decreased detection of *attempted* intrusions. This could be addressed by looking at access requests that were either successful, or unsuccessful, or similar access requests, some of which were successful and some of which were not. Any "chaff" – access requests by their very nature *must* be unsuccessful – are distinguishable from other access requests (either benign or malicious), and that can be put to work for detection.

On a different tack, we can amortize the cost of going through the unique requests. When we look at the logs for the three months following our November log, we see that they make on the order of the same number of unique requests in themselves, but that many of these requests are similar to the ones in the November file. Table 4.3 lists the number of previously unseen requests for the months following November. Studying the requests themselves, many of these only differ in a single component compared to their November counterparts, and are easily dispensed with. Thus the number of unique requests we have to process decreases nicely as we learn more and more about our particular web server. If one has encoded the knowledge of uninteresting subtrees and patterns that were discarded in previous investigations, then this number can be reduced even further. It would be interesting to investigate how these requests should be visualized to maximize the benefits of this amortization process.

Month	New access requests
November	200000
December	87000
January	66000
February	40000

Table 4.3. Number of previously unseen (new) accesses for the following months

Empirically in our data set the uninteresting access patterns are almost without fail very treelike in appearance, with no common tails to speak of, while the opposite is true for the attacks. The reason seems to be that attacks that show some diversity nevertheless share common features that may come at any position in the request, while this is not true for normal accesses. In the case of the encoding attacks against IIS that we see it is the "payloads" i.e., the commands that the attacker wishes to execute, that show many similarities—greater similarities in fact than the encoded path that leads to it. In the case of the spam attacks, it is the stereotype message delivered that is the key to the late similarities. We conjecture that this would probably be difficult to avoid for both types of attacks, there are only so many different commands to execute with the desired effect, and only so many file system paths to get to them, so there is bound to be a bottleneck (where the paths converge to a smaller set, and the command set starts), giving the characteristic hour glass shape. In the case of the spam attack the attacker could randomize the message as well, but that would not elicit the same response from the recipient (human provoked responses are the best indication of a 'live' address the would be spammer could hope for). As there are only so many short sensible messages available, the attacker would either have to generate them by hand, in which case there wouldn't be as many (as the randomly generated addresses at least), or try and generate them automatically, again leading to less diversity. So the hour glass shape is likely to occur in one form or another there as well. On the other hand the access to static legitimate web pages is of course highly tree-like in nature, and hence does not elicit the same hour glass shape. Cgi-bin arguments show more variation, but they don't in our experience contain the same clearly identifiable tails as the attack patterns. In one example, the case of a collection of scripts for conducting surveys of student opinion for courses taken, the text of the messages, while sharing many words between different opinions, still display much more variation, giving an almost random appearance, not the typical hour glass shape of the suspect patterns. However, not all attack patterns show this hour glass shape. The attacks with very little variation in the attack types do not provide enough data for the pattern to emerge. It should be noted that being subject to a large number of different variations of the same kind of attack *increases* the possibility of the attack being detected with our scheme, since there is more structure apparent. The opposite is typically true of signature based intrusion detection systems have been programmed to detect one type of attack (or at least a smaller range of attacks). Diversity in attack method is *good* from our perspective.

A disadvantage with this approach compared to that of automated intrusion detection systems is that the detection is not necessarily real time or near real time. Especially if is decided to visualize the log in batches of one month at a time. Of course, nothing prevents the operator from performing the visualization more often. The methods developed here must be modified for this to work though, as we depend to some extent on having diversity available to visualize, diversity that may not be present in the shorter run. Some form of visualization of the differences between what we have seen previously and what is new since then must be studied. This problem is analogous to the amortization visualization mentioned earlier.

7.   Future Work

The discussion has been limited to the *types* of different attacks seen in the web log (the same request string could emanate from many different sources). No attempt has been made to correlate the actual attacks with each other, or cluster the same attacks originating from different sources to try and identify the entity behind the attacks. Methods to do so already exist, and a visual method is discussed in Chapter 7.

It would be interesting to devise methods of evasion as noted above, and implement the suggested improvements to the log reduction to thwart them. It would also be interesting to devise user experiments. These are more difficult than one might at first think, since training on the specific tool often is very effective for the outcome, and the task to be performed is complex and demands some skill. This makes the experiment prohibitively costly.

8.   Conclusions

In summary, the hypothesis that the combination of anomaly based log reduction and visualization would provide us with the benefits of both approaches while counteracting the drawbacks was supported. Furthermore the anomaly based log reduction system could indeed be very simple and still successfully serve as a front end to the visualization system. The hypothesis that visualizing the structure of the requests strings themselves cut into components would enable the operator to discard benign accesses with relative ease was supported. There was less evidence for the corresponding hypothesis: that one could just as easily identify malicious patterns. A few meta classes of attacks did exhibit features that set them apart from the benign traffic, but others did not to a significant degree.

The presented method is relatively time efficient, and the operator learns about the usage of the website. Notably unusual but benign (often dynamic) traffic that is more varied and hence more prone to misclassification is studied in more detail.

The work invested in parring down the graph can be amortized over subsequent investigations, where the webserver logs for the following months contain less and less new traffic, and hence can be visualized more quickly, especially if one remembers what accesses were seen previously and why it was decided to discard them as uninteresting.

9. Further Reading

There has not been much research into anomaly detection of web accesses besides that by Kruegel et.al. [KV03]. They develop (as is done here) ad hoc statistical methods for detecting anomalous request strings. Their model is much more complex than the one presented here, taking many more parameters into account while only one (the element frequency) is taken into account here. As a result—as far as false alarm rates can be compared between a detector and a log reducer—they are rewarded with a false alarm rate about a factor of forty lower than the one reported here (and possibly a detector that is more resistant to evasion attempts). Even so the authors report a problem with handling even this level of false alarms, while the visualization method presented here enables the user to quickly discard the uninteresting entries.

Chapter 5

COMBINING A BAYESIAN CLASSIFIER WITH VISUALIZATION: UNDERSTANDING THE IDS

In this chapter[1] we aim to develop an intrusion detection system to help the expert quickly and accurately identify false and true alarms. We aim for the expert user as it should be noted that the operator of any intrusion detection system *must* have a rudimentary understanding of the assets that need protection and common ways of attacking said assets.

In order to investigate this approach a prototype tool was developed where the state of a *Bayesian classifier* is visualized to further an understanding, by the operator, of exactly *what* the intrusion detection system is "learning", and how that affects the quality of the output–e.g. in the form of false alarms. To ascertain the effectiveness of the approach, an empirical study of the access requests made to a fairly large public webserver was made, using the same data studies in the previous chapter.

1. Automated Learning for Intrusion Detection

We have implemented an automated learning intrusion detection system that for the sake of accuracy builds a model of both benign and malicious behavior. Automated learning can be roughly divided into two major groups, *supervised* and *unsupervised*. Most anomaly based intrusion detection systems fall into the latter category, i.e. they automatically find clusters or other features in the input data and flag outliers as anomalous. Relatively little investigation in *intrusion detection system research* has been into the area of supervised automated learning systems, [Pro03] being one exception.

Major problems with all self learning systems are the issues of *over training*, i.e. where the system gains a too specific knowledge of the training set, which

---

[1]This chapter is a revised and extended version of [Axe04a].

prevents it from correctly generalizing this knowledge given slightly different stimuli, and *under training* where the system has really seen too few examples on which to base any well founded decision about later stimuli but still classifies as if it had. A goal of our approach is that the visualization of the inner workings of the intrusion detection system will let the operator easily detect instances of over and under training, so as to be able to deal with them interactively.

2. Naive Bayesian Detection

We have chosen to implement an intrusion detection system based on the principles of Bayesian filtering in the same vein as now popular spam filtering software, popularized by Paul Graham [Gra02].[2]

These simple classifiers operate as follows: first the input is divided into some form of unit which lends itself to being classified as either benign or malicious (in spam classifications typically a piece of email is considered), this unit of division is denoted a *message*. It is the responsibility of the user to mark a sufficient number of messages as malicious/benign beforehand to effect the learning of the system. The system is thus one of *supervised* self learning. The message is then further subdivided into tokens—in an email typically the words of the text that makes up the email and various elements of the header. The tokens are scored, such that the score indicates the probability of the token being present in a malicious message, i.e. the higher the relative frequency of the tokens occurrence in malicious messages, relative to its occurrence in benign messages, the more indicative the token is of the message being malicious. The entire message is then scored according to the weighted probability that it is malicious/benign, given the scores of its constituent tokens.

One can parameterize the scoring of the tokens in a number of ways. We have chosen a simple method that closely follows Paul Graham's presentation:

Let the total number of benign messages seen thus far be denoted by *good*, and the total number of malicious messages be denoted by *bad*. Furthermore let the number of times the token has appeared in benign and malicious messages be denoted by g and b respectively (i.e. if it has appeared twice in the same malicious message that is counted as two occurrences). Then the score of the *token* is calculated as: $score = \frac{b/bad}{b/bad + g/good}$. If both b and g are zero then $score = 0.5$, i.e, if we have not seen the token before, then it is given a neutral score of 0.5, meaning that it is indicative of neither a benign nor a malicious message. The *token score* is furthermore restricted to the range $[10^{-9}, 1-10^{-9}]$, to prevent division by zero when the entire *message* is scored. A token is thus never considered *perfectly* indicative of a benign nor a malicious

---

[2]It should be noted that this rudimentary form of Bayesian learning should not be confused with Bayesian learning network algorithms such as employed by the intrusion detection system eBayes [VS00].

message, even though the scores will be referred to as a *perfect* 0.0 or 1.0 for clarity in the remainder of the chapter. It should be noted that one does not actually mark *tokens* as being benign or malicious, only messages. The score of the tokens is *inferred* from the number of times it occurs in benign and malicious messages.[3]

The entire message is scored according to the following formula:

$$p_{malicious} = \prod_{i=0}^{n} p_i / (\prod_{i=0}^{n} p_i + \prod_{i=0}^{n} (1 - p_i))$$

where n is the number of tokens in the message and $p_1, \ldots p_n$ are the respective scores of the tokens.

So the score of the message (i.e. probability the message is bad) is the weighted probability of the probabilities that the tokens the message consists of are indicative of a bad message.

In order to apply this principle to an intrusion detection system, one would typically present it with examples of malicious and benign activity and then when the system is trained, present it with unknown input, flagging all messages that scored higher than a set *threshold score* as intrusive. A more elaborate approach is taken here as will be seen in Section 4.

3. The Experimental Data

For the experiment, we have chosen to study a webserver access log as described in Chapter 4, page 49.

Even though the choice was made to study webserver logs the longer term aim is that the general approach developed here should generalize to other monitored systems. It should be noted that the tool is agnostic in this respect, placing few limitations on the form of the input data.[4]

As mentioned in Bname, there is a dearth of publicly available corpora suitable for intrusion detection research, and the *de facto* standard, based on the Lincoln Labs intrusion detection system evaluation [LGG⁺98] (despite its flaws [McH00]), is unavailable to us as it is export controlled. Other publicly available data such as the Defcon *Capture the Capture-the-Flag* data is not analyzed, and hence it is difficult to base any investigation into the hit/mis-rates of

---

[3] As the dependent probability is never actually calculated (due to efficiency concerns, we would then have to consider the new token given the probability of all preceding tokens, which would lead to a state space explosion) calling this method *Bayesian* is a bit of a misnomer but is standard nomenclature.

[4] That said, lower level, more machine oriented logs may not be the best application of this method. Even when converted to human readable form they require detailed knowledge of e.g. protocol transitions etc. Of course, fundamentally the logs have to make sense to someone somewhere, as any forensic work based on them would otherwise be in vain. Another problem is that of message sequences where the sequence itself is problematic, not one message in itself as the Naive Baysian classifier does not take the *order* of tokens into account.

an intrusion detection system (or train an intrusion detection system) on it. The same is true of anomaly based systems with which to compare our results. We feel it would be pointless to compare our approach to a signature based system e.g. Snort ("http://www.snort.org") because it relies on external knowledge in the form of intrusion signatures that a human analyst, external to the system, has provided.

The university departmental webserver under study was running Apache version 1.3.26. It was set to log access requests according to the *common* log strategy. The log thus consists of a line based text file with each line representing an single HTTP access request. The fields logged were *originating system* (or IP address if reverse resolution proves impossible), the *user id* of the person making the request as determined by HTTP authentication , the *date and time* the request was completed, the *request* as sent by the client, *the status code* (i.e. result of the request), and finally the *number of bytes* transmitted back to the client as a result of the request. The *request* field is central. It consists of the request method ("GET", "HEAD", "CONNECT", etc), followed by the *path* to the resource the client is requesting, and the method of access ("HTTP 1.0", or "HTTP 1.1" typically). The *path* in turn can be divided into components separated by certain reserved characters [FGM+99] .

Recall again from Chapter 4that the log for the month of November 2002 has previously been studied in detail. The resulting access log contained *circa* 1.2 million records. Cutting out the actual request fields and removing duplicates (i.e. identifying the unique requests that were made) circa 220000 unique requests were identified. It is these unique requests that will be studied in the rest of the chapter.

The reason the unique *types* of requests are studied instead of the actual request records is that we are more interested in the *types* of attacks that are attempted against us than the particular instance of the attack. This provides a degree of generalization even in the setup of the experiment as there is no risk of learning any irrelevant features that are then (perhaps) difficult to ignore when trying to detect new instances of the same type of attack later. Note that an entity, e.g.. a worm, that lies behind an actual attack often uses several types of attacks in concert.

Chapter 7describes a method for correlating attacks against webservers to find the entity behind them when one already knows of the particular attack requests being made. It should be noted that no detection capability is lost in this way, since knowing the type of attack being performed it is trivial[5] to detect the instances later, should one chose to do so. The choice was made to

---

[5]The one type of attack that we can think of that would not be detectable is a denial-of-service attack making the same request over and over. Since this would be trivial to detect by other means this is not seen as a significant drawback.

ignore the result code as many of the attacks were not successful against our system, and the result codes clearly demonstrated this. Ignoring this information actually makes our analysis more conservative (it biases our analysis toward false negatives).

Not all possible attacks against web servers would leave a trace in the access log, e.g. a buffer overrun that could be exploited via a cgi-script accessed through the *POST* request since the posted data would not be seen in the access log. Unfortunately the raw wire data was not available; there is nothing really preventing the use of the intrusion detection system on that data, after some post processing. It should be noted however, that few current attacks (targeting web servers that is) are of this type (see Chapter 7) and that there were a multitude of attacks in the access log data with which to test the intrusion detection system.

4. Visualizing a Bayesian IDS

An important problem with self learning systems is that they can be opaque to the user of the system, i.e. it is difficult for the user to ascertain exactly what has been learned and hence to judge the quality of the output. The problems of not really having the human in the loop when making decisions using decision support systems has been noted in human-machine interaction circles for some time [WH99, RDL87]. The operator that does not have a relatively correct (or at least consistent) mental picture of the state of the machine he or she is interacting with will not perform well, probably resorting to ignoring the system he is put to monitor. This problem has also affected anomaly detection systems before, where several systems tested on the Lincoln Labs data (discussed in section 3) seemed to operate well within parameters, but in fact picked up on idiosyncratic differences between the malicious and benign examples in the synthesized data instead of features that would hold were the systems subjected to realistic data [MC03]. It is possible that this effect would have been discovered sooner had the actual learning done by the systems been more accessible to the operators.

The problem is further complicated in the case of intrusion detection because of the base-rate fallacy described in Chapter 3, i.e. that most alarms will tend not to be a true indication of malicious activity unless the intrusion detection system has a very low false alarm rate. Hence the correct identification of false alarms is crucial for the operational effectiveness of an intrusion detection system. Bayesian self learning systems are not immune to these problems if employed in a naive fashion, i.e. when the system is trained in a "batch" fashion, where it is first presented with several examples of intrusive behavior and then several examples of non-intrusive behavior, to finally be applied to unknown input, delivering only (in the worst case) *alarm/no alarm* as output to the operator. A natural improvement is to display the score to the operator, but in practice this is only slightly more helpful. As anecdotal evidence we submit the following:

when the author first started using the Bayesian spam filter recently added to the *Mozilla* ("http://www.mozilla.org") email client, the filter seemed to learn the difference between spam and non-spam email with surprisingly little training. It was not until some rather important email was misclassified as "spam" that it was realized that what the filter had actually learned was not the difference between spam and non-spam, but between messages written in English (by the second author) and the first author's native tongue. In fairness given a few more benign examples of English messages the system was successfully retrained and was again correctly classifying email, but some rudimentary insight into exactly what the system had learned would have made us more skeptical of the quality of the classification, even though the classifier seemed to operate perfectly judging by the output.

To that end a (prototype) tool named *Bayesvis* was implemented to apply the principle of interactivity and visualization to Bayesian intrusion detection. The tool reads messages as text strings and splits them up into the substrings that make the tokens. In the first version of the tool URL access requests make up the messages, and they are split according to the URL field separating characters (; /? : @&=+ , \$) but with little modification the tool could accept any input data that lends itself to being split into messages (perhaps marking sessions) and tokens according to its textual representation. Figure 5.1 is a screen dump of the user interface of the tool.

The learning that is performed by a Bayesian system of the kind modeled here, is encoded in the score of the tokens the intrusion detection system uses to score the messages. Therefore the scores of the tokens are visualized as their textual representation (black text) on a heatmapped background [Tuf01]. A heatmap maps a real number (in our case the probability of the token being indicative of a malicious message, i.e. $p = [0, 1]$) to a color on the color wheel, from green via yellow to red that is, the hue of p—in HSV coordinates—is mapped onto the range $[180^o, 0^o]$, fully saturated, and as close to the whitepoint as possible. The total score of the message is visualized in the same manner and also an indicator of whether the user has marked this message as benign or malicious.[6] One would think that color blindness could be a problem in accessing our visualization (some two to eight percent of all males suffer from defective color vision depending on the group under study—impaired color vision is relatively more common in academia for example), but it turns out that making a simple modification; mapping onto the 'right' half of the color wheel, from green to red via blue, instead of via yellow, will make the presentation

---

[6]Unfortunately the human eye is much better at discerning between different colors than levels of gray, so a gray scale mapping for the purpose of this presentation is less effective at conveying the nature of our visualization. It is suggested that the figures be viewed in the on-line, color version.

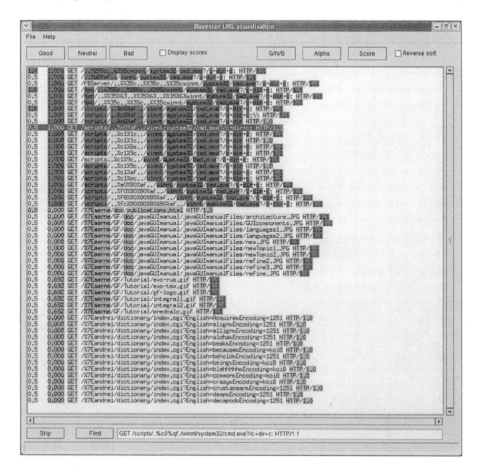

Figure 5.1. The *Bayesvis* tool

accessible to a large percentage of those that suffer from the common forms of red-green color blindness [Tuf01]. This variation is not yet implemented.

Once the user has visual access to the internal state of the classifier, and hence can start to form an opinion of the learning process, it is tempting to let the user interactively guide the learning process, in our case by marking messages on screen as either malicious or benign. In order for this to be practical, the experience must be seamless; ideally the user should not experience any delay between her action and the time the result is displayed on the screen. With a few notable exceptions this requirement has been met and the updating of the state of the messages is instantaneous on reasonably current hardware.

In order to present the ideas embodied in the prototype we give a quick presentation of the user interface, as *user interaction* is its *raison d'être*. The

user interface can be divided into a few major groups roughly corresponding to
the controls from top left to right, top to bottom in Figure 5.1.

Saving/loading Via the file menu, the user can save and load a session, but
   more importantly append new messages (imported as text files) to the end
   of the current session. The user can also clear the actual messages from
   the current session, but keeping the tokens and their scores. This enables
   the user to append new data for classification, without having the display
   cluttered by the training data.

Marking messages The main window of the display lets the user select messages by left clicking on them,[7] and marking them as either *good*, *bad*, or
   neutral. By default the messages are marked as neutral when first imported.
   The display is divided into three columns. The first contains a marker that
   display the state of the message: 0.0, 0.5 and 1.0 depending on the message
   being marked *good*, *neutral* or *bad* respectively on a heatmapped background. The intended mnemonic is the score the resulting tokens would
   have, were they part of only one message of the indicated type. The second
   field is the Bayesian score of the message (also on a heatmapped background), indicating the relative *"badness"* of the message as a whole. The
   third column fills the rest of the horizontal screen estate and consists of a
   heatmapped display of the tokenized message. The characters that separate
   the tokens, and hence are not part of the scoring process (they have no score
   of their own) are also displayed, but on a white background. This serves
   to separate the heatmapped tokens from each other visually, and to provide
   the original data, without fooling the user into thinking that the separating
   characters are somehow part of the detection process. The user can choose
   to display the actual scores of the tokens in curly braces after the tokens
   themselves.

Sorting The user can opt to sort the messages alphabetically (optionally in
   reverse order), but perhaps more interesting is the ability to sort according
   to message score. Since this tool provides a visual display of the scores in
   descending order, a cut-off score as in an anomaly based intrusion detection systems has not been implemented. Instead users can sort messages
   according to score and view them in order, deciding for themselves when an
   uninteresting level has been reached. The last sorting option is the option
   to sort according to the marking of the messages, with the ordering *good*
   < *neutral* < *bad*. This is useful during a training or scoring session to
   quickly find misclassifications inxxmisclassification (messages with a *good*

---

[7]A range of messages can also be selected by click dragging or shift clicking, which is useful when we are
training the system on a large corpora of already know malicious accesses as we are in this paper.

(green) score that one has marked *bad* (red) will stand out visually among the correctly classified messages). The sorting functions in general and the sorting of scores in particular are exceptional in that they do not provide an instantaneous response like the other functions of the system – although the response time is still reasonable.

Searching At the bottom of the screen is an ordinary sequential search function. More interesting is the *skip* capability used for skipping similar messages, especially when dealing with semi tree like data as is done here.

In Figure 5.1, a few examples of bad and good access requests have been loaded. The user has marked three malicious requests as malicious (which can be seen in the left most column) and one request as benign. As a result all malicious requests have been correctly classified as malicious (they all have a perfect 1.0 score), and most of the benign requests have been marked as benign. A few toward the bottom of the page still have a high score (having a score of 0.692), and the next step would be to mark the first of them as benign and see how that would influence the rest of the misclassified requests. Figure 5.2 displays the Bayesvis after this update has been made.

It is interesting to note that had a batch oriented system been trained with these examples and just the scores been observed we could well have been pleased thus far as all the other benign requests have a perfectly benign score of 0.000. However, when looking at the heatmap of the tokens of the last requests it becomes clear that the reason behind this is the token "1.0" which receives the perfect 0.0 score, and this dominates the score of the request as a whole. As it happens, in the requests upon which the system was trained the token "1.0" appears once, in a good message, and never in a bad message, and this serves to give it a perfectly *benign* score. As the system has never seen any of the other tokens in the requests they default to a score of 0.5, which is to say that they are not indicative of anything. To the human analyst using the tool, it is abundantly clear that the last requests here are correctly classified more by coincidence than anything else. The system does not really have enough input yet to say with any reasonable degree of certainty that these requests are benign, and more training is called for. Figure 5.3 shows Bayesvis after the first of the under trained accesses have been marked as benign.

Contrast this training of benign requests with the malicious requests. As it happens just marking the first request in Figure 5.1 correctly classified all the malicious requests. In this case it is because of the tokens of the payload, i.e. the tail of the request that tries to execute a command interpreter on MS Windows operating systems (see section 5 for more details of this type of attack). A few more requests were marked to increase the level of training of the tokens that precede the payload. In this case it is quite apparent to the operator that the detection is of a higher quality given the training set, since the tokens that

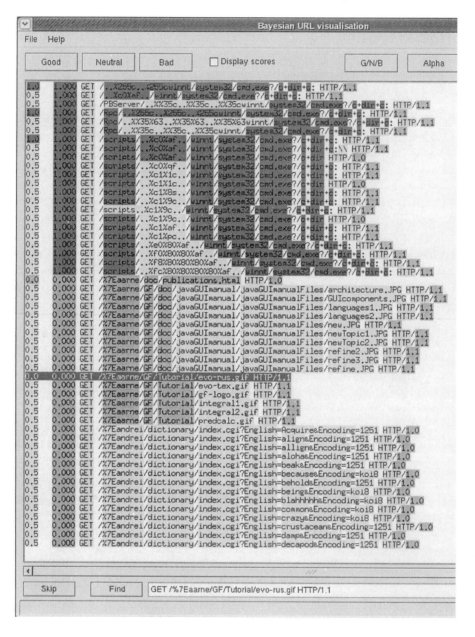

Figure 5.2. The *Bayesvis* tool after retraining on false alarms

are marked are quite significant given the type of flaw that is being exploited.
In this small example, the strengths and weaknesses of the learning process

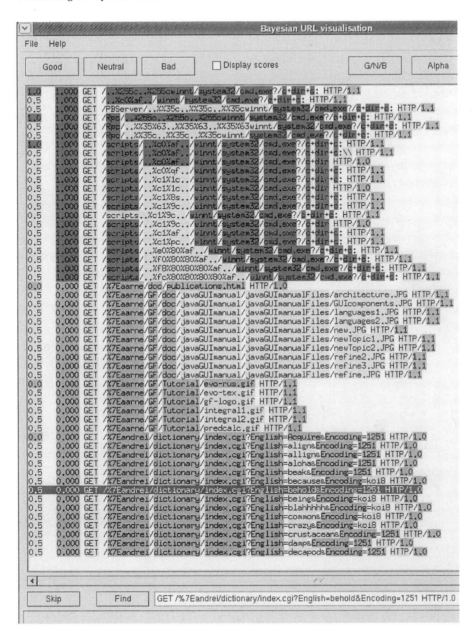

Figure 5.3. The *Bayesvis* tool after having corrected under training

become visually apparent, and the operator can respond interactively to correct the instances of *under training* seen, in doing so receiving immediate feed back (*click-by-click* literally) and taking into account the new state of the intrusion detection system, before performing additional updates. This would not be true of a more traditional intrusion detection systems working along the same lines.

Figures 5.1, 5.2, and 5.3 contain more information as to under and over training, such as the benign indication for the "1.0" token on some of the malicious requests and the continued malicious indication for the "1.1" token. Unfortunately the static nature of a written presentation, prevents of from providing more insight into the interactive nature of this process than possible here[8]

5.   The Training Data[10]

We previously sifted thorough the November 2002 access log by hand, classifying each of the 216292 unique access request for the purpose of intrusion detection research.

It was decided to classify the accesses into two categories, *suspect* and *intrusive*. The reason for using a *suspect* class is that since this is data from the field, and we do not know the intentions of the entity submitting the request, it is sometimes difficult to decide whether a request is the result of an intrusive process, the result of a flaw in the software that submitted it, or a mistake by its user. Also, some accesses are just plain peculiar (for want of a better word), and even though they are probably benign, they serve no obvious purpose. On the one hand the *suspect* class consists of accesses that can acceptably be brought to the attention of the operator. But on the other hand, as they are not proper indications of intrusions, we accept that they may not be reported as intrusive.

The classification of the attacks was described in detail in chapter 4. In summary, table 5.1 details the number of different types of access requests in the training data.

6.   The Experiment

The choice was made to train the system on the November log with the identified weaknesses mentioned above[11] and then to evaluate the resulting intrusion detection systems on the logs for the following months. Examining the logs for the months following November, i.e. December through February, we note that they contain on the same order of number of unique requests in themselves, but it turns out that many of these requests are similar to the ones in the November file. However the number of accumulated previously unseen requests for the following months fall off nicely: November 200000, December

---

[8]*Bayesvis* is available under the General Public License.

[10]These attacks are described in more detail in Chapter 4 beginning on page 49They are summarised here for completeness.

[11]It is perhaps unreasonable to assume that every operator of such a tool should do their own security evaluation to acquire training data, but of course nothing prevents training the system on malicious data made available by an external expert, much like intrusion signatures for signature based intrusion detection systems are typically subscribed to from an external provider.

Access meta-type	Unique requests
Formmail	285
Unicode	79
Proxy	9
Pathaccess	71
Cgi-bin	219
Buffer overrun	3
Miscellaneous	7
Total attack requests	673
Normal traffic	215504
Suspect	115
Total requests	216292

Table 5.1. Summary of the types of accesses in the training data

87000, January 66000 and February 40000. In addition, studying the requests themselves, many of these only differ in a single component compared to their November counterparts, and hence ought to be easily dispensed with. Thus the number of unique requests that have to be processed decreases nicely as more knowledge about our particular web server is accumulated. As we are only interested in the type of attack, the system will only be tested on the reduced logs where previously seen requests have been filtered out.[12]

6.1 Training

Since an interactive tool with feedback is tested, several possible strategies for training present themselves. A strategy was chosen that is believed to be biased toward *detection*, i.e it will result in as high a detection rate as possible at the cost of more false positives. The strategy is to mark all the previously identified malicious requests as malicious and then mark the false positives as benign until there are no obvious ones left. We name this strategy: *Train until no false positives*. The cut-off score for the URL is set at 0.5 (which is conservative), i.e. a score above 0.5 for a benign access request is considered a false positive. This strategy is in contrast with a strategy that would add more examples of benign activity by actively searching for them and marking them as benign, even though they may not have a score that would make them

---

[12]The reduction itself was performed by judicious use of the *sort, uniq,* and *comm* commands.

false positives in our eyes. For examples of other strategies and their merits in training Bayesian spam classifiers see [Yer04].

Figure 5.4 shows a detail of a step in the early phases of the training, where all the attacks and suspect accesses have been added and marked, but the operator has yet to perform much in the way of correcting false alarms. As seen in the picture, all the accesses are either yellow or red, with tokens such as *GET* being highly indicative of a malicious access. It is not difficult to realize that this would probably not hold for a sufficiently trained intrusion detection system, as the majority of all requests are *GET* requests. Hence, the operator starts by marking a few of the benign accesses (one is selected ready for marking in the picture). When a few accesses have been marked the operator can re-score, re-sort and repeat the process, until the false positive rate is at an acceptable level, according to the strategy described above. To give an indication, for the November data set it turns out that only 325 accesses need be marked before there are no false positives.[13] This should be contrasted with the total number of malicious/suspect accesses marked ($673 + 115 = 788$) and the total number of benign accesses (215504). Thus, only a small fraction of the benign accesses need be marked as benign for the false positive rate to reach acceptable levels for this data set.[14] Due to the nature of Bayesian classifiers, this does not result in perfect training, three accesses have a score above 0.5 even though they have been marked as *benign* as they are short and contains suspect tokens only. It should be noted that it is fully expected that the false positive training is somewhat fragile, i.e. the system will not give the benefit of the doubt to new access requests, that even though they are benign are sufficiently dissimilar to the ones marked, as the system does not have a great deal of benign data from which to generalize any notion of benign accesses.

6.2   Evaluation

The evaluation consists of erasing the training data, saving the tokens with their respective scores and loading the access requests for the next month. Then the accesses are sorted according to URL score and the URLs with a score surpassing our threshold 0.5 is judged for false positives, and the ones with a lower score for false negatives.

---

[13]We feel compelled to point out that the time taken to accomplish this task is of course trivial. If the user is to have any hope of evaluating the output of *any* intrusion detection system, then he or she should not have to spend more than 10 seconds per access request at the very most (probably much less) which means that the training would take less than one hour.

[14]Even though it is less likely that we could rely on external security knowledge for the training on benign data than on malicious data, as the benign data is by its nature site specific, this is not as problematic as the site operator *must* have an idea of what data the site provides. One also should not discount the possibility that there is some potential for crossover between benign data for different sites due to e.g. directory structures, templates etc. being similar for similar server software in use at different sites, and thus external benign data might still make useful training data.

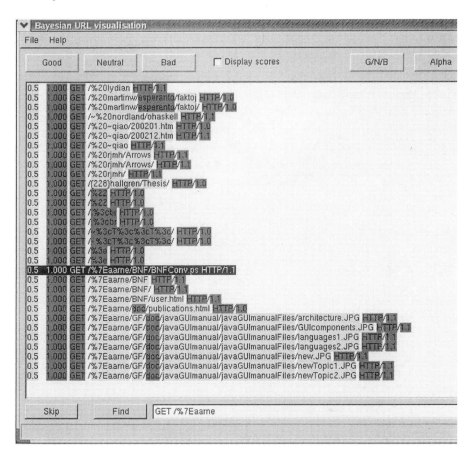

Figure 5.4. False positives during the training phase

Indeed as suspected, latter results (see Figure 5.5) show some false alarms. Here the visualization of the internal state of the intrusion detection system displays its strengths. We see that similar "~andrei" URLs have clearly been marked as benign some time earlier, as much of them are green, but a few instances of the tokens (in this case input to a cgi-script that translates phrases between English and Russian) must have been part of malicious accesses earlier, since they have a perfect score of 1.0, being thought to be highly indicative of malicious accesses. In this case, the majority of the URL consists of benign tokens, and the relatively low score (most proper alarms have a perfect score of 1.0) makes it clear that these are in fact false alarms. As it happens, marking just a handful of these accesses as benign (containing the tokens: *root*, *not* and a few others) suffices to bring the score of these requests well below the threshold. This process is simplified by the instantaneous update of the display. As the first URL is marked (bringing down the score of the *not* token), all other URLs that contain that token are immediately updated, with their corresponding total score. The operator then chooses the next URL that has not been affected and mark that one, receiving instantaneous feedback on how that affects the rest of the false alarms. This is a level of interactivity that (at the time of writing) we have not seen in any other intrusion detection system tool, though it is unfortunately difficult to do justice to in this presentation.

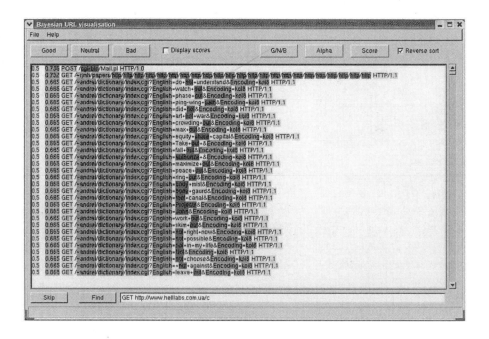

Figure 5.5. Examples of false alarms in February log

A third example of the detection process is given in Figure 5.6, where the generalization capabilities of the intrusion detection system are demonstrated. Here we see several examples of Unicode attack Unicode type attacks that have not been seen beforehand, which is illustrated by the number of yellow (i.e. not previously seen) tokens. Despite this all the attacks are correctly classified as malicious, since they contain the typical Unicode payload or a variation thereof. The intrusion detection system manages to generalize the learned detection capability for this type of attack (this turns out to be true for the other classes as well) and it is easy for the operator to convince herself that these alarms are genuine, as they contain several highly significant suspicious tokens. To give an indication of the generalization capability; in the January data alone Bayesvis detected on the order of 200 generalized Unicode attacks.

We conjecture that it would be difficult to avoid detection for this type of attack. There are only so many different commands to execute with the desired effect, and only so many file system paths to get to them, so there are bound to be a few significant tokens that will show up in all such attempts. We also believe it would be difficult to drown the operator with *chaff* i.e. attacks that looked similar on the surface but with extraneous tokens generated more or less at random. Since one could opt not train the system on these attacks (marking them neither as benign or malicious), their tokens would not pollute our token frequency tables and hence they would receive a much lower score than the true attacks as shown here. As the detector was not trained on much benign traffic, trying to drown the malicious tokens by injecting (conjectured) benign tokens would not help much either, since it would be difficult for the attacker to guess exactly which few of the possible tokens that signify a benign message. (Several recent spams try to fool the detector using this very approach). As this is a side effect of our training strategy, other strategies may display other characteristics.

6.3   Results

While a summary of the performance of the Bayesian detector itself fails to capture the interactive aspects of the intrusion detection tool, table 5.2 contains the approximate counts of the instances of true and false alarms and the *suspect* accesses that were classified as benign. As the system was progressively retrained on the false alarms in the files in question the quality of the detection increased. It was always relatively easy to identify false alarms, as these typically had relatively many tokens of a benign or neutral nature, with only one or two indicative of maliciousness, hence the number of false alarms as seen in Table 5.2 does not say as much about the ease (or difficulty) with which these could be identified. The only exception to this rule is were the access requests consist of only one or two tokens in total. If these tokens happen to be part of a malicious request, then marking and re-scoring would not tend to change the status of the misclassified request as a whole, since there simply was not enough data to work with. If the request consists of just one biased token, Bayesian classification cannot do much. This is of course a problem for all such classifiers, and one that becomes readily apparent from the visualization of the requests. As conjectured, the detection rate was impressive, with no missed true attacks, though it should be pointed out that the analysis performed was *not* as thorough as that which lead to the November training data. The mis-classifications, i.e false negatives, that did crop up where all in the *suspect* class, and in line with the discussion in Section 5 they are not considered missed attacks. In summary

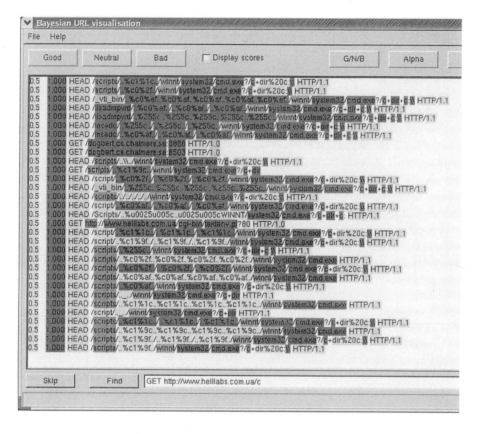

Figure 5.6. Generalized detection of Unicode attacks

we have processed access logs containing close to 5 million access requests[15] (divided onto more than 400000 unique types of accesses) in two to three hours including the one hour to initially train the system (discounting the time taken to find the malicious examples). This time does not differ to a substantial degree from the time the user would have to spend on going through the output of a traditional intrusion detection system with similar performance as our Bayesian detector.

7. Conclusions

We have developed an intrusion detection tool based on Bayesian classification. The tool—*Bayesvis*—provides the user with interactive visual feedback on the state of the learning process, and as such the user can both ascertain the

---

[15]This is a realistically sized example, though it cannot measure up to the likes of e.g. *Google*.

Month	Unique req.	True alarms	False alarms	False neg. suspect
December	87000	700	20	15
January	66000	560	40	20
February	40000	240	10	10

Table 5.2. Summary of the results of the experiment (approximate values)

quality of the output (by viewing the process that give rise to the alarms) and selectively train the system until it has reached a sufficient level of learning.

The tool was tested on our own corpora consisting of four months worth of access requests to a fairly large university department web server, using a *Train until no false positives* strategy. The tool proved successful. The Bayesian detector was somewhat successful in correctly classifying requests as intrusive or benign, and the visualization made the limitations of the detector and the training readily apparent to operator who could evaluate the quality of the output and re-train the intrusion detection system interactively as necessary. One user of the tool could well handle logs containing close to five million access requests in the same amount of time it would take the operator to process the output of a traditional intrusion detection system, with the added benefit of being able to easily and interactively tune the intrusion detection system.

Furthermore, the training itself proved to not be unreasonably time consuming if one discounts the time taken to identify malicious examples to train the system on, a task that can be carried out by external experts and amortized over several installations as is the case with signature based intrusion detection systems today.

Chapter 6

VISUALIZING THE INNER WORKINGS OF A SELF LEARNING CLASSIFIER: IMPROVING THE USABILITY OF INTRUSION DETECTION SYSTEMS

1. Introduction

Current intrusion detection systems are difficult to use. The more advanced systems apply machine learning principles to help the user avoid manual labor e.g. in the form of having to write intrusion signatures. However, the more advanced such systems become, the more *opaque* they become. By *opaque* we mean the difficulty with which the user can discern what the system is doing. With such self learning systems it becomes very difficult for the user to correctly judge the quality of the output of the system, e.g. by correctly identifying false alarms [WH99]. As false alarms can be the constraining factor for intrusion detection (see Chapter 3) this is an important problem.

In the preceding chapter we described a visualization method for the state of a self learning intrusion detection algorithm, to lend the user greater insight into what the system was learning. This aim includes, for example, helping the user detect instances of over training and under training, and enabling the user judging the veracity of the output of the system. However, the algorithm visualized then had several shortcomings: it was a relatively simple algorithm that does not take the order or context of tokens into account. For example, the classifier cannot learn that the tokens "A" and "B" in isolation are indicative of a good context, but that the tokens 'AB' in conjunction are indicative of a bad context. To address these shortcomings and to see whether visualization methods could be successfully applied to a more complex classifier, with a more complex state to visualize, we describe an IDS prototype based on a more complex and capable classification algorithm.

The detector was applied to two corpora of data: our own, consisting of web server access requests, and a subset of a data set with system call traces. We also compared the detector to the less advanced one described in the previous chapter. The detector performed well enough for the purpose of demonstrating the visualization capabilities and these helped the user correctly differentiate between false and true alarms.

2.   Markovian Matching with Chi Square Testing

We have modeled the detector after popular and successful spam detectors [MW04, Yer04] since these have a number of desirable traits:

- They are self learning and need only be presented examples of desirable and undesirable behavior.

- They build a model of both desired and undesired behavior instead of building models of only one or the other and thus have a potential advantage when it comes to detection accuracy.

- They can detect behavior in streams of data that may only exhibit some local structure, a very open ended detection situation.

- Spam classification and intrusion detection share similarities and these detectors have performed very well in the spam classification scenario.

Training and classification begins as follows: first the sequence is divided into records and the records into tokens. Then a sliding window of length six is moved over the tokens, one token at a time. For each sliding window position, a set of *features* is formed. This feature set is the set of all subsequences obtainable by replacing some but not all tokens by the distinguished blank token "⟨skip⟩".

An example will make this clearer: Consider the record "The quick brown fox jumps over the lazy dog" with the individual words as tokens. First the window is slid across the input, the first window being: "The quick brown fox jumps over." Then the feature set is formed: "⟨skip⟩ ⟨skip⟩ ⟨skip⟩ ⟨skip⟩ ⟨skip⟩ over", "The ⟨skip⟩ brown ⟨skip⟩ ⟨skip⟩ over" etc. such that all possible combinations are covered.

The feature set is isomorphic to the powerset of the six tokens (assuming that they are distinct), minus the empty set. Thus for a window of size six, there are $2^6 - 1 = 63$ features per window.

A weight (W) is then assigned to each feature according to the formula: $W = 2^{(n-1)}$ where n is the number of non-⟨skip⟩ tokens in the feature. The weights are *superincreasing*, so that the weight assigned to a long feature (i.e. one that contain many tokens and less empty positions) outweighs all of its subfeatures combined. This way we approximate (piecewise) a Markov model instead of actually attempting to generate a proper unified Markov model.

Training of the classifier consists of running examples of good and bad records through the above process and counting the number of times the resulting features occur in a good and bad context respectively.

Classification i.e. assigning a score to each record is similar but here we begin by using the resulting frequencies from the previous step to calculate the *local probability* (P_l) of the feature being indicative of a bad context. The probability is calculated by the following formula: $P_l = 0.5 + W(n_b - n_g)/2(n_b + n_g)$ where n_b is the number of times the feature occurs in a bad context, n_g is the number of times the feature occurs in a good context and W is the weight as described above. The formula for P_l is purposely biased towards 0.5 for low frequency counts, such that features that do not occur often are not considered as indicative of context as features that have higher frequency counts. Thus, somewhat simplified, P_l indicates the *badness* of a feature on a sliding scale from 0.0–1.0. With $1 - P_l$ indicating the *goodness* of same feature. Of course, 0.5 means that we either found equal evidence for the feature indicating a good or bad context, or no evidence at all. So far the detector is heavily influenced by Yerazunis's *Markovian matching* [Yer04].

Given the local probabilities of the features P_l they have to be combined into an overall score for the entire record (P_s). We have chosen here to perform a chi square test as done in the SpamBayes project [MW04]. The local probabilities of all features are tested against the hypothesis that the message is good and bad respectively and these probabilities P_g and P_b are combined as: $P_s = (P_g - P_b + 1)/2$. The detector proper returns P_s, P_g and P_b for later visualization.

The choice of using a window length of six merits further discussion. Yerazunis original detector (CRM-114) has a window length of five, but no further insight into why that choice was made is provided [Yer04]. In a sense a longer window size would be better, as that enables the detector to detect order dependent features further apart. However, with superincreasing weights, these longer features will also serve to make the relative weight of the shorter features lower, which means that the detector might make a misclassification having learned a long irrelevant sequence that drowns all shorter sequences. There is also the issue of the runtime of the detector. As we calculate the feature set of the window, the size of the set is exponential in the number of tokens, so a longer window means much more data to learn or classify. To keep the runtime reasonable a window length of six was chosen. Furthermore it has been demonstrated that the data from Warrender et. al. [WFP99] require a window length of at least six to detect all intrusions in that dataset, and as we will later illustrate, the ability of the detector to classify based solely on the ordering of tokens with examples from that data, it seemed appropriate. It should be noted though that the particular window size of six seemed to be an artifact of one particular trace of the Warrender experiment, and not based on any deeper underlying feature of the nature of the intrusive or normal processes [TM02]. In any case this issue merits further attention, especially considering that the attacker ought to be considered to know the window length used.

3.   Visualizing the Detector

A problem with the detector described in Section 2 as it stands is that it is *opaque* to the user of the detector. When training the detector the user get little or no feedback on what exactly the detector is learning and how to improve on the situation. When using the detector for scoring unknown data the user does not get much insight into *why* the detector classified the way it did. This makes it difficult to discern when the detector is operating correctly and when it is not, i.e. identifying false alarms and missed detections. Our hypothesis is that visualization of the state of the detector with interactive feedback when training will lend the user insight into how the detector is operating and thus mitigate these problems.

The straightforward approach we have described in the previous chapter, the *bayesvis* tool, is to display the token stream one record line, and color code the tokens in some way to signal their significance to the user. A problem here is that the detector proper divides the input stream up first into windows and then into features, and this is clearly too much data to display on one line. Applying the visualization idea of *Overview and detail* [CMS99, pp. 285–305]—where one part of the display gives an overview of the data and another part more detail about the region of interest—seems appropriate. The visualization problem is one of devising a workable overview display, i.e one that summarizes the detail data in a consistent manner such that the user can discern which records are worth a closer look and which are uninteresting.

Figure 6.1 is a screenshot[12] of the prototype visualization tool *Chi2vis*. The data displayed are HTTP access request strings that will be discussed in greater detail in Section 4. From a visualization standpoint it is divided into three panels showing progressively greater detail the further towards the bottom of the screen the user looks. The bottom most panel displays the scoring features of the currently selected window. The middle panel displays all windows of the currently selected record and the top panel displays the records.

Starting at the bottom of Figure 6.1, we describe the components of the interface in turn:

Feature Panel The *feature panel* displays the relevant features in two columns (made up of one *score column* and six *token columns* each) with the left column sorted on P_l in ascending order (the column marked *score* in the

---

[1] Where the lower part of the display does not contain any data the figures have been cropped.

[2] Unfortunately the human eye is much better at discerning between different colors than levels of gray, so a gray scale mapping for the purpose of this presentation is less effective at conveying the nature of our visualization. It is suggested that the reader consults the original figures, aviable from "www.cs.chalmers.se/~dave/VisBook", or the on-line, color version

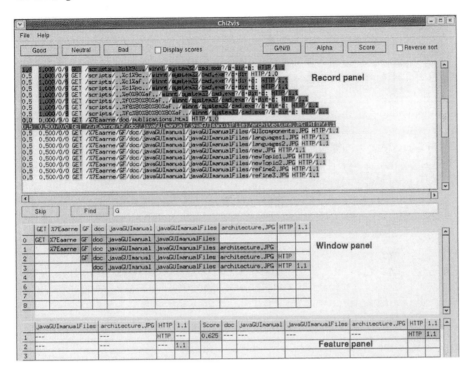

Figure 6.1. The *Chi2vis* tool after training one bad and one good (Cropped)

panel) and the right column sorted in descending order.[3] Thus the left column displays the feature most indicative of a good record at the top and the right column displays the feature most indicative of a bad record at the top. The features themselves are displayed one to a line on a heatmapped background [Tuf01], i.e. the color is mapped on the color wheel from green for $P_l = 0$ via yellow for $P_l = 0.5$ to red for $P_l = 1.0$. The color chosen is at the rim of the wheel, i.e. it is fully saturated and with a maximum value. This way the greener the feature the more indicative of a good context, and conversely the redder the more indicative of a bad context. The actual numeric score of the feature is also displayed to the left of the feature itself. It should be noted that these features are the only features displayed that are actually taken into account when the detector proper scores a record.

Window Panel The middle panel, the *window panel*, displays the windows of the currently selected record in such a way as to give the user both the

---

[3]Note that only the right column is fully visible in the figure i.e. it has all six token columns and the score column visible. Only the rightmost four token columns of the left column is visible.

opportunity to select a window[4] for display in the feature panel and to give an overview of the feature values for other windows not currently selected. In order to do this we have chosen to use the chi square test as in the detector, but here on a token by token basis. For each token in the window each feature in the database is extracted and all features that have the same token in the same position are selected. The local probability values of these features are then put to the chi square test and the combined score of the test determines the hue (i.e. on the green–red scale) of the heatmapped background color. The hypothesis probabilities P_g and P_b are combined into a single value (summed) and that value determines the saturation (i.e. how close to the whitepoint; at greater saturation, further from the whitepoint, the colors appear less "washed out") of the heatmapped background. In this way the user can discern two parameters: how good/bad indicative the word is and how certain the detector is of that classification, with a high degree of certainty (i.e. P_b low and P_g high or vice versa) producing a saturated color and a lower degree of certainty producing a more washed out appearance.[5] If the word never occurs in any feature then the background color is set to gray which serves as a marker that this token has not been seen before.

Record Panel Lastly the *record panel* at the top is visualized much the same as the window panel, i.e. the relevant features are extracted and combined as for the window panel but now each word can of course be part of multiple windows as well. It should again be noted that it is only the feature probabilities that are actually part of the scoring proper. The chi square tests performed in the window and record display are designed to give the user a consistent summary of the actual scoring/learning process.

The interaction with the training phase is via the three top most buttons (or their keyboard shortcuts) whereby the user can mark a record (or range of records) as being *good* or *bad* examples (or resetting them to *neutral* status in case of error).

A few other fields in the record view deserve mention. The leftmost column is a marker that displays the training status of the record (0.0 on green background for *good*, 0.5 on yellow background for *neutral* or *untrained* and 1.0 on red background for *bad*). Next is the total score of the entire record on a heatmapped background (with certainty value taken into account) rounded to three decimal places, then P_g and P_b for the record mapped onto the range 1–9 (i.e. one

---

[4]In the window panel of the figure, detection window number three has been selected as is indicated by the blue outline of the first element ("doc") of that window. The whole record is not marked more clearly as that would obscure the heatmap. Unfortunately that is not the case for the record display as that is not possible with the graphical user interface toolkit used.

[5]These parameters are not completely independent. A score of 0.5 could never occur with a really high degree of confidence for example.

character each) on a heatmapped background (from yellow to green and yellow to red respectively) and finally the record itself as previously mentioned.

To aid in both training and using Chi2vis as a detector the user has several options regarding sorting the record view. The user can sort on *good/neutral/bad* i.e. the training status of the records, on the records alphabetically, and also the record according to the record score.Of course the user can also save/load etc the session or by removing all the currently loaded records but keeping the feature data, save the resulting detector and load new records to be scored without having the display cluttered with old training data. The user can also search in the data by was of the *find* and *skip* buttons that find the search string indicated or skip ahead to the next record that *does not* match the search string (counting from the beginning) respectively. To facilitate search and skip the feature was added that when the user clicks on a record the record is copied from the beginning up to the character under the cursor to the search field. If the user wishes to see individual token scores (as abstracted above) she can select *display scores* which will included them in brackets after the tokens themselves. This also displays the total score (and confidence values) in the status bar with full precision in addition to the rounded values presented in the record display itself.

It is of course difficult to do justice to the interactive qualities of a tool such as this in a static presentation, but to give a feel for it a small example is presented in the screenshots in figures 6.1, 6.2 and 6.3. A few examples of malicious and benign web access requests have been loaded into Chi2vis. The issue of malicious and benign web access requests is discussed in more detail in section 4. In the first screenshot (Figure 6.1) the user has marked one access request as bad and one access request as good. As we can see the training is actually adequate for the attacks, Chi2vis correctly marks all the other examples of attacks as malicious. (For added detection accuracy perhaps more examples should be trained on in an operational setting). This is seen not to be the case for the benign access requests though, the detector finds insufficient evidence to be sure of the status of most of them. As we can see in the figure, this is due to the detector inadvertently thinking that requests that end with the pattern "HTTP 1.1" are malicious (In typical use the irrelevant tokens learned are not of this trivial nature, they have been chosen here for purpose of illustration). This is of course not likely to be true, indeed looking at the training data this seems indeed to be a fluke in that the one good example does not contain the "HTTP 1.1" pattern though the other misclassified benign access requests do. In Figure 6.2 the user has thus selected and trained another benign access request and that has served to make the detector correctly classify the other visible benign access requests. However, in the same figure we spot the reverse situation where the "HTTP 1.0" pattern has likewise been found to be indicative of a good context, even though the overwhelming evidence of a bad context has sufficed to make the correct classification in this instance. However, as the pattern in itself is known to not materially affect the outcome of any attack the user selects the offending access request to retrain the tool. Figure 6.3 displays the situation after the update. In this figure we can see that the "HTTP 1.0" pattern (and all permutations) in themselves have been reevaluated to have a 0.500 score, i.e. neutral. In conjunction with the attack access request though (as we can see in the lower right part of the figure) it is still indicative of a malicious request, which is as it should, as the classifier has learned the essence of the attack: the attempted invocation of a command interpreter and hopefully the many variations thereof.

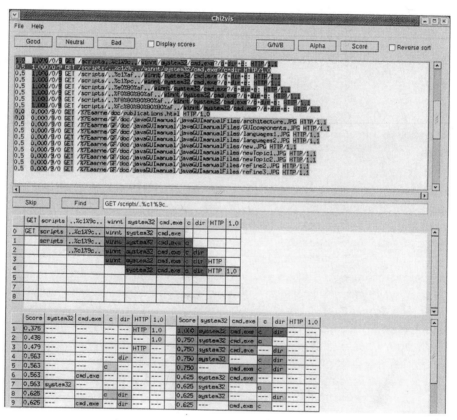

Figure 6.2. The *Chi2vis* tool after training one bad and two good

Note that the display of the summary data in the two topmost views (even though this data is not actually part of the scoring) seem to work well. From the bottom up they give a progressively less detailed picture of what the detector has learned, providing a useful overview of the detailed lower level data, without cluttering the display with irrelevant information.

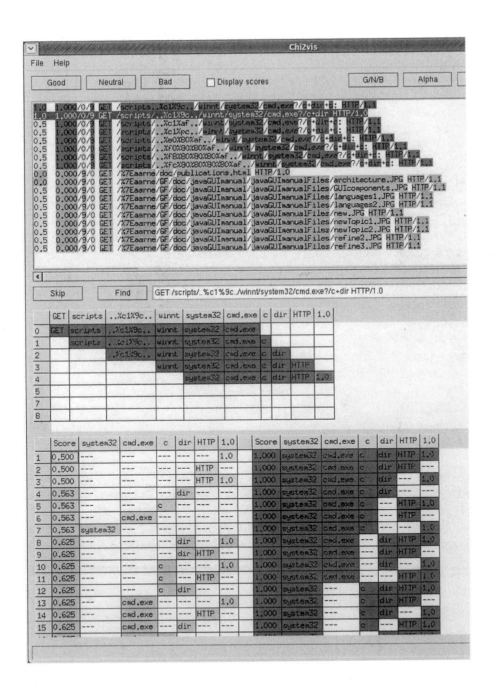

Figure 6.3. The *Chi2vis* tool after training two bad and two good

4. The Experimental Data[7]

We have chosen to conduct two different experiments. The first more comprehensive experiment is on our own web server access log data, and the second on publicly available order dependent system call trace data described in [WFP99].

For the first experiment we used the same data as the preceding chapters (Chapter 4and Chapter 5), based on a webserver access log .

Even though the choice was made to study webserver logs, the longer term aim is that the general approach developed here should generalize to other monitored systems. It should be noted that the tool is agnostic in this respect, placing few limitations on the form of the input data.[8]

The log consists of a text file with each line representing an single HTTP access request. The fields logged were *originating system* (or IP address if reverse resolution proves impossible), the *user id* of the person making the request as determined by HTTP authentication, the *date and time* the request was completed, the *request* as sent by the client, *the status code* (i.e. result of the request), and finally the *number of bytes* transmitted back to the client as a result of the request. The *request* field is central. It consists of the request method ("GET", "HEAD", "CONNECT", etc), followed by the *path* to the resource the client is requesting, and the method of access ("HTTP 1.0", or "HTTP 1.1" typically). The *path* in turn can be divided into components separated by certain reserved characters [FGM+99] .

The log for the month of November contained circa 1.2 million records. Cutting out the actual request fields and removing duplicates (i.e. identifying the unique requests that were made) circa 220000 unique requests were identified. It is these unique requests that will be studied.

We had previously gone thorough the November 2002 access log by hand, classifying each of the 216292 unique access request for the purpose of intrusion detection research.

The data that resulted was described in more detail in Chapter 4 and are only summarized briefly in Table 6.1. The table details the number of different types of access requests in the training data.

---

[7]The description of the data here, save for the description of the Warrender system call data at the end of the section, is similar to the more detailed description in Chapter 4, beginning on page 49. They are summarized here for completeness.

[8]That said, lower level, more machine oriented logs may not be the best application of this method. Even when converted to human readable form they require detailed knowledge of e.g. protocol transitions etc. Of course, fundamentally the logs have to make sense to someone somewhere, as any forensic work based on them would otherwise be in vain. Another problem is that of message sequences where the sequence itself is problematic, not one message in itself.

Access meta-type	Unique requests
Formmail	285
Unicode	79
Proxy	9
Pathaccess	71
Cgi-bin	219
Buffer overrun	3
Miscellaneous	7
Total attack requests	673
Normal traffic	215504
Suspect	115
Total requests	216292

Table 6.1. Summary of the types of accesses in the training data

The system call data from Warrender et. al. [WFP99] consists of long runs of system call names (without arguments) E.g. *mmap:mprotect:stat:open:mmap:-close:open:read* etc. Figure 6.6 illustrates this further. The interesting aspect of this data is that the number of tokens (different system calls) is quite small and that they all occur in all traces. Hence it is solely the *order* of the system calls that differentiate a good trace from a bad trace. Unfortunately this also makes them less suitable for this type of detector as there is less data available for the user to make sense of visually. Nevertheless we deemed it interesting to see how the detector proper performs when subjected to such data as it is order dependent only, and it was furthermore the only such data that was available. A problem here is the lack of intrusive data with which to train the detector. The original *stide* detector developed by Warrender et. al. [WFP99] used in the experiments was a pure anomaly detector in that it only learned benign patterns and flagged patterns sufficiently abnormal as an intrusion.

5. Experimental Results

We have conducted three experiments of the effectiveness of Chi2vis. The first two with the data described in section 4 and the last is a comparison with the Bayesvis detector described in Chapter 5applied to the same web access requests as Chi2vis is here.

5.1 Web Access Requests

For the first experiment we partitioned the web access request data described in section 4 into a set of training data and a set of test data. Ten percent of the accesses (with a minimum of one access request) in all the classes of attacks and the normal data were selected at random. The *suspect* access requests were not included. The detector was then trained on all the resulting training attack access requests (i.e. they were all loaded into Chi2vis and marked as *bad*). The normal training data was added and enough of the normal data was marked as good until no false positives were left. This was accomplished by repeatedly re-sorting by score and mark the worst scoring requests as *good*. We call this strategy: *Train until no false positives*.   A request was considered a false positive if it had a displayed score of 0.500 or higher. A total of 280 access requests had to be trained as *good* until all false positives were gone.

It should be noted that for many of the attack types, one might suspect from the outset that too few training examples were provided (i.e. only one example), as we can see in Table 6.2.[9] This is not as much of a draw back as expected though, as this experiment is mainly about illustrating the viability of visualization as a means of understanding what the detector is learning, and less about illustrating to what extent such a detector could be made to perform well. As we can see in table 6.2, the two classes where more than twenty examples were presented performed reasonably, with one of the classes that contain fewer examples (seven for the Unicode-class) does admirably. Viewing a sample of the access requests themselves in Figure 6.4 it becomes apparent that this is probably the class most suitable for intrusion detection training as it consists of a well defined type of attack that is easy to differentiate from benign access requests. Note that the system has correctly picked up on the "attack tail" of the requests, i.e. the system interpreter that the access request ultimately seeks to execute. While the command interpreter invocations in the data are not completely identical in all instances, the learning of the features with less tokens also serves to identify them. In Figure 6.4 we see the very head of the path (_vti_bin) also playing a role in the detection.

As for the experiment described in Chapter 5, we conjecture that it would be difficult to avoid detection for this type of attack since certain significant tokens are inevitable. We also believe (as we argued previously) that it would be difficult to drown the operator with *chaff*. For example, as the detector was not trained on much benign traffic, trying to drown the malicious tokens by injecting (conjectured) benign tokens would not help much either, since it would be difficult for the attacker to guess exactly which of the possible tokens that signify a benign message. As this is a side effect of our training strategy, other strategies may display other characteristics. We concede though that this area merits further attention.

---

[9]The various classes the attacks have been divided into are also probably more or less suitable as a classification for detector training.

Access meta-type	Training	Testing	False eg.	False neg. (%)
Formmail	28	257	0	0
Unicode	7	72	2	3
Proxy	1	8	2	25
Pathaccess	7	64	34	53
Cgi-bin	21	198	15	8
Buffer overrun	1	2	1	50
Miscellaneous	1	6	3	50
Total	66	607	57	9
Normal	21550	193954	-	-

Table 6.2. False negatives (*misses*) in testing data

The features detected in this data were all within the window length chosen. The attack tails for the Unicode attacks for example were all around length five. The detector would still have been able to detect the attacks with a shorter window as the tokens themselves do not occur in the normal data, but had they occurred the detector with the current window length would still have been able to detect them given the unique order of tokens in the execution of the command interpreter.

The *raison d'être* of Chi2vis though is in helping the operator identifying false alarms (false positives). Fortunately for us there were a few false alarms with which to demonstrate the capabilities of the visualization. Table 6.3 details the false alarms. Looking at Figure 6.5 we see that the five false alarms that begin with *HEAD* form a pattern. The detector has obviously seen evidence that the pattern "HEAD ⟨skip⟩ ⟨skip⟩ HTTP 1.1" is modestly indicative of an intrusion. And looking at the training data it is relatively simple to spot these attack patterns. However, in this case it is clear that the detector has been over trained on the attack pattern (or indeed under trained on the normal pattern) and marking only one or two of these patterns as good in this context serves to bring the pattern in question to a more normal score while still not compromising the detection capability of the detector as can be seen by looking at the already trained attacks Doing so reduces the number of false alarms from 30 to 4 in the test data.

5.2   Warrender System Call Trace Data

The second part of the experiment uses a subset of the available traces from Warrender *et. al.* mentioned earlier. The data chosen are the normal *login* traces

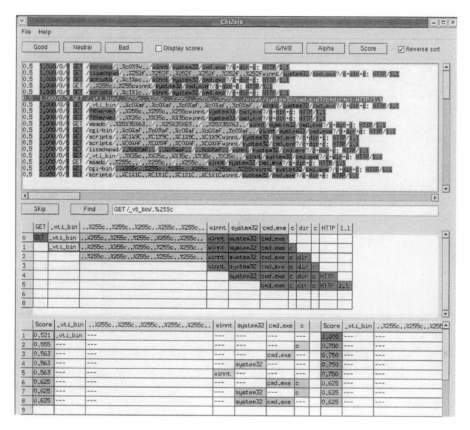

Figure 6.4. Generalising the Unicode training to detect new instances

Type	False alarms	F.a. (%)
HEAD-pattern	26	0.010
Others	4	0.002
Total	30	0.015

Table 6.3. False positives (*false alarms*) in testing data

and the "homegrown" attack traces from the *UNM login and ps* data[10] with those traces that only contain one system call removed. More data sets are available but as the visualization part of Chi2vis is less useful on this data, and the time

---

[10]Available at the time of writing at "http://www.cs.unm.edu/~immsec/data/login-ps.html".

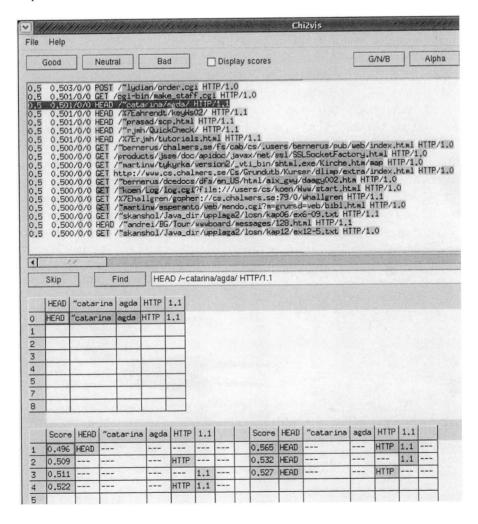

Figure 6.5. False alarms: Example of the *HEAD*-pattern

taken to train and evaluate the detector on such long traces (several thousand tokens each) are substantial, only one data set was chosen for evaluation.

The data was converted to horizontal form with one trace per line for inclusion into Chi2vis. There were, unfortunately, only a total of 12 traces of normal data, and 4 traces of intrusive data in the data set chosen. Access to more traces would have been preferable. A complication with this data is that the intrusive traces (naturally) contain long traces of benign system calls. As a consequence of how the detector in Chi2vis operates we cannot hope for the intrusive traces to be given a high score (close to 1.0) as there will be substantial evidence of normal behavior in them. Thus we will have to consider a low score (close to

0.0) as benign and a higher score (0.5) meaning that there is evidence of both good and bad behavior, to signify an attack.

Using interactive visual feedback as a guide, training the detector on 4 good traces and 2 bad traces (unfortunately a substantial part of the available intrusive traces) yields a detector where 10 of the good traces are correctly classified and 2 of the good traces are not (i.e. false alarms). Likewise 3 of the bad traces are correctly classified but 1 of them is not (i.e. missed detections). Note that these figures *include* the training data. Thus while the detector does not operate splendidly, given the lack of training data, there is some evidence that it can differentiate between good and bad traces in the Warrender data. Figure 6.6 is a visually rather boring illustration of this. It has been cropped to illustrate the relevant overall results. In the figure the good traces were prepended with the character "?" and the bad with "@" for illustration (they are not part of the training).

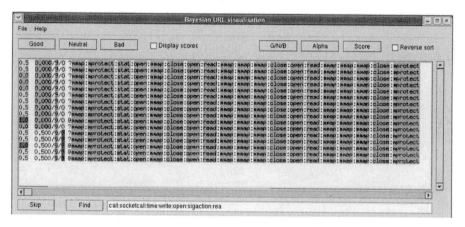

Figure 6.6. Results from training on syscall data (Cropped)

It should be noted that we do not suggest that Chi2vis would make a good choice of detector for this type of data. As it has had the arguments to the system calls removed there is not enough context for the operator to be able to evaluate the classifier. Thus this kind of data is not a good match for a detector with a visualization component. We evaluate Chi2vis on this data set as it is the only data available to us where the difference between malicious and benign behavior is solely in the order of the tokens.

5.3   Comparison with Bayesvis

As it would be rather pointless to develop a visualization of the more complex detector presented here if it faired worse on the same data set than our previous attempt described in Chapter 5, we present a comparison of Bayesvis and Chi2vis in this section. The visualization portion of Bayesvis is based on the heat mapping principles presented here, but the detector proper is based on a naive Bayesian classifier, which is simpler than the detector applied here. Most notably naive Bayesian classification does not take the order of the tokens into account when classifying, instead treating every token in isolation. To investigate the differences between these two detection principles we present the results of subjecting Bayesvis to the data in section 5.1. As Bayesvis does not take the order of the tokens into account it would be pointless to compare its performance on the Warrender data in section 5.2.

We trained Bayesvis on the same data according to the same principles. In doing so we had to mark 67 access requests as good in order to bring all the benign access requests in the training data below a total score of 0.500. This should be compared with the 280 access requests we had to mark benign until Chi2vis was sufficiently trained. We conjecture that this is because Bayesvis due to its less sophisticated detector is more eager to draw conclusions from what might be less than sufficient data.

Table 6.4 details the false negatives (misses) of Bayesvis on the data in this paper.

Access meta-type	Training	Testing	Chi2vis	False neg	False neg (%)
Formmail	28	257	0	0	0
Unicode	7	72	2	0	0
Proxy	1	8	2	5	63
Pathaccess	7	64	34	51	80
Cgi-bin	21	198	15	17	9
Buffer over-run	1	2	1	2	100
Miscellaneous	1	6	3	5	83
Total	66	607	57	80	13
Normal	21550	193954	-	-	-

Table 6.4. False negatives (*misses*) in testing data for Bayesvis

As we can see it performs substantially worse overall than Chi2vis. One data point deserves further mention though. The 51 misses in the *pathaccess* category can be divided into $9 + 42$ misses of which 42 are of the same category, a short "HEAD" access request with the total score of the request being 0.490 (i.e. barely benign) owing to the "HEAD" token having a score of 0.465. Just marking one of them as malicious marks all of the remaining 41 access requests as bad (total score 0.587 with the "HEAD" token score of 0.563). However, as this goes against the *train until no false positives* strategy on the original benign data we have refrained from doing so. We would furthermore have to go back to the benign training and see that this update did not have a detrimental effect on the other categories (both in terms of false negatives and positives). Looking at the individual access types, Bayesvis does better in only the *Unicode* category. We hypothesize that it is because Bayesvis has an easier time generalizing from the example access requests in this rather straight forward category, as it interprets what evidence it has more liberally, while Chi2vis is hampered by not having seen sufficient evidence to be able to classify them as malicious. If this line of reasoning is correct, Bayesvis eagerness to classify requests as malicious on what might be less than solid evidence ought to show up in a higher false alarm rate for Bayesvis than for Chi2vis.

Table 6.5 and Figure 6.7 details the false negatives (false alarms) in the benign testing data.

Type	Chi2vis F.a.	Bayesvis F.a.	Bayesvis F.a. (%)
"cgi-bin"-pattern	-	20	0.010
Others	-	21	0.011
Total	30	41	0.020

Table 6.5. False positives (*false alarms*) in testing data for Bayesvis

As we can see our hypothesis of a higher false alarm rate was corroborated. Even if the false alarms were dominated by one pattern (the "cgi-bin" pattern detailed in Figure 6.8) as was the case for the Chi2vis experiment (though Chi2vis false alarms were dominated by a different pattern), the remaining false alarms still outnumber Chi2vis by a factor of two. Retraining could rectify the "cgi-bin" token problem but doing so is more problematic here than in the case of the Chi2vis "HEAD" pattern discussed earlier. In that case we were certain we were only affecting the short benign requests by retraining but here we would affect *all* requests that contains the "cgi-bin" token benign as well as malicious.

In summary, Bayesvis does at least slightly worse in almost all respects compared to Chi2vis on the web access request data. One exception might be the benign training where Bayesvis required substantially less examples of benign behavior before a sufficient level of training was accomplished. We conjecture that this is a consequence of the simpler detector requiring less evidence before "jumping" to conclusions, as supported by the higher false alarm rate.

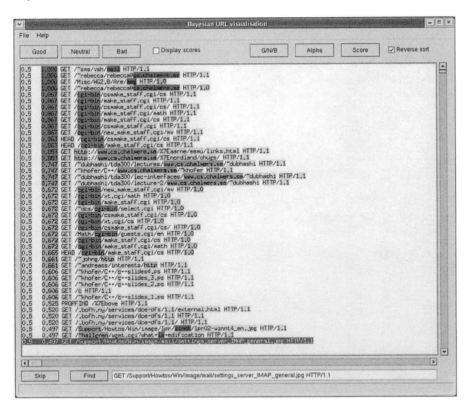

Figure 6.7. All the false alarms of Bayesvis

We are not aware of any other attempts at visualizing the state of a Naive Bayesian (or similar) classifier than that of Becker et. al. [BKS01] which describes a product in the SGI *MineSet* data mining product by the name of *Evidence Visualizer*. Becker proposes to visualize the state of the Naive Bayesian classifier in a two pane view where the prior probability of the classifier is visualized as a pie chart on the right, and the possible posterior probabilities for each attribute on the left as pie charts with heights, the height being proportional to the number of instances having that attribute value. The second display can also be in the form of a bar chart with similar (but not identical) information, where, to quote from the article:

> [The] Naive Bayes algorithm may be visualized as a three-dimensional bar chart of log probabilities [...] The height of each bar represents the evidence in favor of a class given that a single attribute is set to a specific value." (Kohavi et. al. [KSD96]).

The display works well for models with a relatively modest number of attributes (which are probably continuous). A classical data set that is used in the paper to illustrate the concepts contains measurements of petal width and length, and

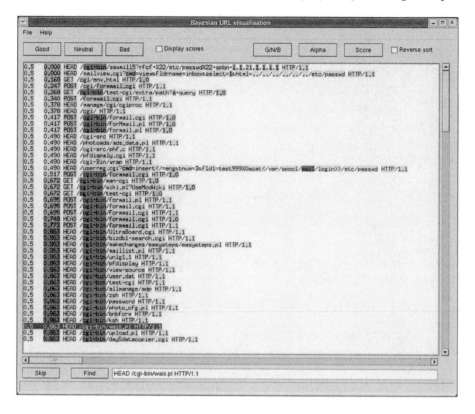

Figure 6.8. The "cgi-bin" pattern false alarms of Bayesvis

sepal width and length for three labeled species of Iris. Thus in this data set there
are only four different attributes. Other data sets in the paper have eight different
attributes. The models we visualize, on the other hand, routinely have *many*
more attributes (i.e. the number of all features seen in training). As such we only
visualize the user selected attributes for which we have values and summarize
the findings at a higher conglomerated level (i.e. we only visualize the selected
features of the selected window that the record contains, visualizing the ones
not present, possibly tens of thousands, would not make sense in our case). We
also visualize the data directly (i.e. the text of the tokens). A similarity with
the visualization presented in this chapter and the previous is that the user of
Evidence Visualizer is provided with feedback on how many instances the model
has been trained on, data that is available to the user with our visualization in the
form of the whiteness of the individual attributes (and as heatmapped scores for
the whole record). As the models the two approaches visualize are so different
and the applicability of the *Evidence Visualizer* to the model presented here is

difficult to judge, it is difficult to compare the two (rather different) visualization approaches further.

6. Conclusions

We have developed a Markovian detector with chi square testing. A method for visualizing the learned features of the detector was devised. As this display was too detailed to be useful in and of itself, a method to visually abstract the features to give the user more overview (in two steps) of the data was developed.

The resulting prototype *Chi2vis* was put to the test on two data sets. A more extensive one comprising of one month worth of web server logs from a fairly large web server and a smaller one with publicly available system call trace data. The experiment demonstrated the ability of the detector to detect novel intrusions (i.e. variants of previously seen attempts) and the visualization proved helpful in letting the user differentiate between true and false alarms. The interactive feedback also made it possible for the user to retrain the detector until it performed as wanted.

7. Future Work

A first step is to develop or gain access to other corpora of log data that contains realistic and known intrusive and benign behavior, and to apply our tool to such data. An investigation of how visualization could be applied to other detection techniques is also planned.

The question of attacks (evasion, injecting *chaff* etc.) against the approach taken here also needs further study as many of the attacks developed against spam classifiers cannot be directly translated to the scenario presented here.

Any human computer interaction research is incomplete without user studies. These are easier said than done however. The process of classifying behavior into malicious and benign using a tool such as ours is a highly skilled task (where operator training would probably have a major influence on the results). It is also a highly cognitive task, and hence difficult to observe objectively. If such studies are to be of value they would almost certainly be costly, and the state of research into how to measure and interpret the results is perhaps not as developed as one might think.

Chapter 7

VISUALIZATION FOR INTRUSION DETECTION—HOOKING THE WORM

1.   Introduction

This chapter[1] explores the possibilities of employing a trellis plot of parallel coordinate visualizations to the log of a small personal web server. The intent was to find patterns of malicious activity from so called *worms*, and to be able the operator to distinguish between them and benign traffic. Several such patterns were found, including two that were not the result of worms and one of which was unknown at the time to the security community at large.

1.1   Worms

Worms (e.g. [Pfl97, pp. 179,192]) are self replicating programs that attack a remote computer system (often by exploiting some weakness) to gain access. They then transfer a copy of themselves to the subverted system and start running there. Once they are established in the subverted system the cycle begins anew, and the worm starts scanning for other systems to infect.

Worms may or may not carry some sort of payload (logic bomb or otherwise) that perform an additional sinister task. The *Code red* worm [CER01a] for example, launched a denial-of-service attack against a fixed IP address (belonging to the "whitehouse.gov" web site) on the 20–27 of each month.

Worms have spread far and wide in the last few years, with far reaching consequences. Often they are combined with viruses i.e. the worm has viral properties also, but not always. The names of the most successful worms have percolated up to the common consciousness, with instances reported widely in

---

[1] An expanded and revised version of [Axe03].

the press and other news media e.g. the outage of *The New York Times* servers when they were attacked by the Nimda worm [USA01].

Worms often exist in several variants, which are smaller or larger variations on the same basic theme. The Nimda worm is reported in five different variants in the wild [CER01b]. Finding different variants of worms, if and when they occur, is therefore interesting from a security perspective, since they may exploit new vulnerabilities that may yet not have been addressed, and for research into the spread of worms.

2.   The Monitored System

We have chosen to take the access log file of a small personal web server, that has been continuously available on the Internet for some months. This web server serves a small number of web pages from the home of the first author, to the circle of his immediate family and close friends.

This web server is perhaps not representative of the majority of web servers on the Internet in that it requires authentication for all accesses. This would of course make it relatively simple in some sense to sort the illegitimate access attempts from the legitimate ones, but we have chosen not to take the result codes of the operation into account in our visualization, and therefore we claim that the study of such a system could be generalized to include systems which do not require authentication.

A perhaps more significant problem is that the web server does not have much in the way of legitimate traffic. It is small and personal, and is only accessed by a dozen people or so. One could argue that this could make illegitimate accesses stand out more, not having much in the way of legitimate traffic in which to "hide". Even so, since we are looking for worms that often account for the majority of the traffic on much larger web sites, we still think the study of such a small system worth while, even though it remains to be seen if the results from this study can be generalized to larger systems. It is interesting to note in this context that the accesses patterns on this webserver is similar to what would be seen on a *honey pot* webserver, i.e. a server set up for the sole purpose of drawing attacks to it in order to study them further.

Even if the method employed here does not scale to much larger web servers when employed directly, we believe it is feasible to combine it with other methods that first reduce the logfile to manageable proportions. Such reduction methods invariably suffer from the false alarm problems mentioned earlier, and hence it is not unreasonable to imagine a situation which is similar to the one here, i.e. that we have a relatively small dataset with a sizable proportion of intrusive activity, mixed with benign access.

The web server runs thttpd, a small, secure and fast web server written and maintained by Jef Poskanzer, see "http://www.acme.com" for more information. At the time of the experiment thttpd had an impressive security record with no published security vulnerabilities. The log records from the web server contain the following fields:

IP address This is the IP-address of the system the request originated from. Thttpd does not have the ability of doing reverse DNS queries, and hence does not have the option of reporting the hostname of the remote system in the way that e.g. Apache can.

Remote username This is ostensibly the username of the (remote) user that the request originated from. We know of no web browser (or other client) that divulges this information.

Authenticated username The username the client provides authentication for. Thttpd (and other web servers) provide for authentication in the form of requesting a *username–password* pair from the originating web browser. If the authentication is successful the authenticated username (i.e. on the web server) is logged. If the authentication fails the attempted username is not logged, instead this field is left blank.

Time The time and date the request was received.

Http request The request string exactly as it was received the client. This is formed by the access method (*GET, HEAD*, etc), followed by the URL of the resource the client requested.

Http status code The status code that was returned to the client. Unfortunately the full list of codes is too long to reproduce here. The interested reader is referred to the HTTP specification in RFC 2616. Noteworthy are the codes: *200* which denotes the successful delivery of the requested page, and *404* which signals the well known "page not found" error.

Number of bytes This is the number of bytes that was sent in response to the request (if any). The HTTP response is not included in the count, only the actual page that was sent. Hence this value is blank for all erroneous requests.

Referring URL If this request resulted from the user clicking a link on another web page, the client has the option of sending the URL of that web page (the "referring" page) as part of the request. Not all web browsers do this (at least not for all requests) so this information is not always available.

User agent The name of the client software, if divulged by same. Note that for compatibility reasons many browsers let the user modify the value sent, to be able to masquerade as using another browser than they actually do. This is to thwart overzealous web designers who for misguided concerns about compatibility only allow certain browsers to access their web site.

An example of a few log entries can be found in Figure 7.1.

```
213.37.31.61 - - [25/Sep/2002:17:01:56 +0200] "GET /scripts/..%%35c../
      winnt/system32/cmd.exe?/c+dir HTTP/1.0" 404 - "" ""
172.16.0.3 - stefan [25/Sep/2002:19:28:28 +0200] "HEAD /sit3-shine.7.gif
      HTTP/1.1" 304 2936 "http://server/" "Mozilla/5.0 (X11; U;
      Linux i686; en-US; rv:1.1) Gecko/20020827"
172.16.0.3 - - [25/Sep/2002:19:28:46 +0200] "GET /pub/ids-lic.pdf HTTP/1.1"
      200 615566 "http://server/pub/index.html" "Mozilla/5.0 (X11; U;
      Linux i686; en-US; rv:1.1) Gecko/20020827"
213.64.153.92 - - [25/Sep/2002:22:57:51 +0200] "GET /scripts/root.exe?/c+dir
      HTTP/1.0" 404 - "" ""
```

Figure 7.1. Sample records from the webserver log file

Thus the log contains a maximum of nine degrees of freedom. In our data set this is reduced to eight, since no web client divulged the remote login name of the user, and hence this field is always empty. All the other fields have values for at least a subset of the records.

The log contains some 15000 records, and begins in earnest on 25 Sept 2002. It ends on 1 Jan 2003, and thus covers some three months of activity. As a comparison, the web server log for the computer science department at Chalmers for the month of November 2002 contains on the order of 1.2 million accesses, comprised of circa 200 000 unique requests.

3.   Scientific Visualization

The security log data has multiple dimensions with no a priori dependent variables and is therefore multivariate in nature. Spence [Spe01, pp. 45] lists only a handful of methods for the visualization of multivariate data. Of these we have chosen the tried and tested techniques of the parallel coordinate plot [Ins97] combined with a trellis plot in one variable [Spe01, pp. 168].

The main reasons for choosing parallel coordinate plots over the other methods were:

- The visualization does not give preference to any dimension at the cost of other dimensions. This is important if we don't have any indication about which data may be more important from the point of view of making a successful visualization of the data set. Other visualization methods give some dimensions of the data a more prominent (visually striking) position at the cost of others.

- Parallel coordinate plots can visualize data with more dimensions than the other methods. It is not unreasonable to visualize data with ten or even twenty dimensions. Most of the other available methods strain when faced with four. As we shall see this turns out to be less important to us as we will reduce the data set to five dimensions. Since our original data set contains eight degrees of freedom, and it would not be unreasonable to visualize them all in an operational setting, the ability to visualize many dimensions is still an important consideration in choosing the visualization method.

■ The visualization methods lends itself to trellis plots, i.e. where we make a plot of plots (see below), in one of the variables. This is an effective method in seeing trends in higher dimensional data, when one variable has been singled out, in our case to group the requests. Not all the other methods lend themselves to trellis plots as well as the parallel coordinate plot, if at all.

■ The parallel coordinate plot is very generally applicable; it can handle both continuous and categorical data (though admittedly some of the key benefits are lost then) and it can be used to both see statistical correlations between data points, and as a more general profile plot, where the appearance of the graph itself (rather than the curve forms as in an ordinary x-y scatter plot) can be used to identify features. We will use the parallel coordinate plot in the latter capacity.

■ The last, but by no means the least, of our considerations is that the parallel coordinate plot is well researched and the theory around it somewhat more mature than is true of many of the alternatives.

3.1 The Parallel Coordinate Plot

We have used the tool Spotfire to make the parallel coordinate plot [2]. A parallel coordinate plot is prepared by taking each data point and projecting it as a line joining the components of the vector onto a set of parallel coordinate axes. This form of visualization does not only let the viewer learn about the dependencies between the variables, but also lets the viewer quickly see emerging patterns, and compare different datasets for similarities and differences [Ins97].

Figure 7.2 illustrates the case where 68 different points in eight dimensional space have been mapped onto (eight) parallel coordinate axes. In this case the dataset was chosen by limiting the log file from our webserver to the first 68 data points. We choose the eight dimensions that had data. They are in order in the figure:

Date The date and time the request was made. In this case the data has been limited by selection, and hence the available dates only cover a small percentage of the axis. Spotfire does not rescale the axis when the visible data is limited in this way, to preclude the effect where abrupt scale changes makes

---

[2]"http://www.spotfire.com"

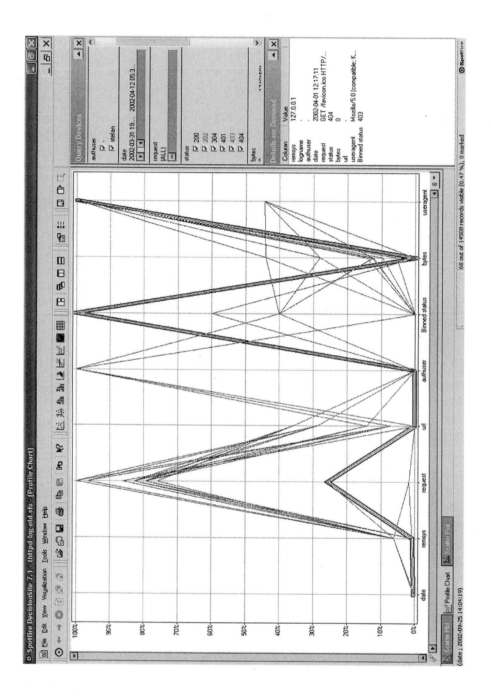

Figure 7.2. A simple parallel coordinate plot

the user lose his orientation as different ranges of data are selected. If we had rescaled manually, or made smaller datafile, then the available dates would have covered the entire axis from 0% to 100%. This is of course true for all the subsequent data as well.

Note the *date* slider, in the *query devices* sidebar, that has been manipulated to select the narrow range of records that are displayed.

Remsys/Request/Url This variables are imported as strings, lexicographically sorted, and plotted as categorical data.

Authuser The username of an authenticated user, or the minus sign if no authentication has been performed. Note the check boxes corresponding to the two possible values in this dataset at the very top of the *query devices* side bar.

Binned status The status (e.g. *404–not found*) that the request resulted in. This data was imported as integers. However the result codes are not integral per se—i.e. magnitude comparisons between the result codes *200* and *404* interpreted as the integers 200 and 404 respectively, makes little sense. Instead the result codes have been rescaled by being sorted into bins chosen so that each result code ended up in a bin of its own. This has transformed the integral data into categorical data which is plotted with each bin equidistant on the vertical axis. The order of the bins is also user selectable.

Bytes The number of bytes that were sent in response to the request. Imported as integers, and in this case the data has a magnitude as opposed to the *status* data. Spotfire has the ability to logscale such data (and many other possible scalings can be applied as well) should the user so chose though we have opted not to.

Useragent Typically the browser that made the request, if that information has been divulged. Imported as a string and hence treated as lexicographically sorted categorical data.

For the purpose of this paper we will not use the possibility of finding correlations between data points using the parallel coordinate plot directly. However, just to hint at the possibilities; in Figure 7.2 we see a strong inverse correlation between the result code (*binned status*) and the *auth user* field, indicating that the lack of authentication leads to "access denied" types of error codes, and vice versa. This is not surprising given that we have already stated that the webserver was configured to use authentication for all accesses. However, we used a similar plot to discover that the access controls had been misconfigured at one point (after having upgraded the webserver) giving access to the world.

It should be noted that while *Spotfire* does not mark the axes with any label indicating the range in absolute terms, hovering the mouse over any specific value displays the coordinate of the axis, as well as all coordinates for the closest record. Data points can also be marked and the data for the corresponding records displayed in the sidebar *details-on-demand*. Here we have marked one record (indicated by the thicker lines surrounding it) and the corresponding record is visible in the lower right corner of Figure 7.2.

Another sidebar (*query devices*) allows the user to dynamically adjust the data that is displayed, e.g. a continuous variable can have a slider (or other user selectable input element) that lets the user select the relevant parts of the data set for display. This sidebar is in the upper right corner in the figure. In this case it displays three examples of query devices: *check boxes*, a *range slider* and an *item slider*.

As these are dynamic user interface properties, it is of course difficult to do justice to their user benefits in a paper presentation.

3.2   The Trellis Plot

The *trellis plot* (or *prosection matrix* in the case of continuous data) is described in [Spe01, pp. 168]. It was originally used as a way of extending two dimensional scatter plots into three dimensions, without introducing a 3D view and all the complications that follow. Instead a pair of the variables is singled out and a plot of subplots is made, typically arranged in a triangular matrix, where the axes represent the different possible choices for the pair of parameters, and the x–y position in the matrix contains a plot of the other parameters for the x–y value of the singled out parameters. In the case of continuous data, it is of course not possible to make a continuum of of subplots. Instead a discrete number of ranges of values of the pair of parameters is chosen and the corresponding subplots made.

In our case, we will chose only one variable, not a pair. We will single out the request string, which is already a categorical entity. Since we only make one parameter choice, the x–y position of the subplot within the trellis plot will not carry any further information—conceptually the subplots would be laid out in a linear fashion one after another—but are laid out on the plane so as to use screen real estate effectively. By doing the trellis plot this way we hope to find similarities in access patterns corresponding to *different* requests, and hence being able to visually cluster them corresponding to the entities (human or worm) that lie behind the particular requests in that cluster. This is also how we use the parallel coordinate plot as a profile plot. It is the profiles ("blobs" if you will) that exhibit similarities between the different subplots and we will use these similarities to group the requests into clusters.

4.   Visual Analysis of the Log File

The aim of this investigation is to find support for the hypotheses that the web server was targeted by some of the more popular worms (that attacked web servers) during the period in question. We would also like to be able to tell apart the different types of worms, if any, and also to differentiate between the access patterns made by worms, and those made by others, i.e. more or less ordinary users. We will perform this by correlating different requests with each other to see if they cluster into patterns of activity that can be distinguished from one another. We wish to make distinctions both between benign and malicious accesses, and also between the various malicious accesses themselves.

There is some justification for the belief that such differences will be present. For example Feinstein et. al. [FSBK03] report differences in the distributions of source IP addresses between automated denial-of-service type attacks and benign traffic. These differences are significant and enables the attacked site (or intervening router) to differentiate between these types of traffic based on source IP address alone.

Since our web server requires authentication it would be natural to divide access into *allowed* and *denied* as a first step, but as we we have mentioned earlier; since most web servers are not configured this way, we will refrain from using this data. Furthermore, since we do not see how this would allow us to tell different *kinds* of worms apart, another approach is necessary.

Attack of web servers typically have to do with exploiting weaknesses in the web server's handling of input data, either by having the server misinterpret it, doing something the designers never intended, or by triggering a buffer overrun, thereby allowing the attacker to take control at a lower level. Since the only real source of input data is the *request* the web client (browser/worm) makes, it is (as we mentioned earlier) natural to make the visualization pivot on the request. We have already mentioned that one way of accomplishing this is to make a trellis plot of the log data, with the request being the controlling variable.

In Figure 7.3[3], a specific parallel coordinate plot has been made for each of the unique request strings (59 in total), i.e. the request string has been held constant, and all data pertaining to other requests have been filtered out in each of the 59 plots. As a consequence the request string was removed from the subplots themselves as it would not add any useful information. In fact it would have detracted from the similarities of the plots since it would have been different for each of the subplots.

---

[3]Here, as for other detailed figures, we refer the reader to the book's web page where full color figures are available: "www.cs.chalmers.se/~dave/VisBook".

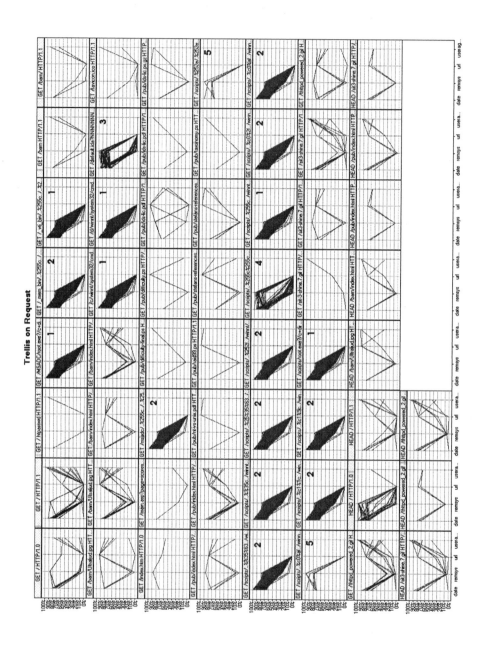

Figure 7.3. A trellis of parallel coordinate plots

In order not to taint the results of the investigation with data that pertains to the success or failure of authentication, we have reduced the dataset to the following four variables:

Date The date the request was made.

Remsys The IP-address of the system that made the request.

Url The referring URL if any.

Useragent The user agent (browser) that made the request, if provided.

The variables *Authuser*, *Status* and *Bytes* had to be removed since they tainted the experiment by leaking information (directly or indirectly) about the success or failure of the authentication:

Authuser The username of the authenticated user, since this would immediately leak information about the success or failure of authentication.

Status The result code that the request resulted in. There is a result code that communicates "authentication failure" and hence that would also directly leak information.

Bytes The number of bytes that was sent. In the case of authentication failure, the webserver would not respond (in the same way as if the authentication would have succeeded), and hence not send any reply as a result of the request. This would set bytes sent to zero, and hence correlate rather strongly with authentication failure (though not perfectly).

Removing data from the visualization actually strengthens the results of the experiment in that we remove security relevant information, making the task more difficult. In an operational setting we most likely would not perform this reduction.

To illustrate the concept in greater detail; Figure 7.4 is an enlargement of the plot marked "3" in Figure 7.3. The axes are labeled with the respective variable.

5. Results of the Investigation

Even a quick glance at Figure 7.3[4] reveals four interesting patterns (marked 1–4 in the figure). Looking closer at the individual plots we can see that they originate from a large number of systems, and dates. They are also comprised of a lot of repetitive accesses (i.e. a large number of records). Other patterns can also be identified, more about them will be said later. They look markedly different even ignoring the fact that they are comprised of much fewer accesses.

---

[4]Or at least at the full resolution color version ("www.cs.chalmers.se/~dave/VisBook")

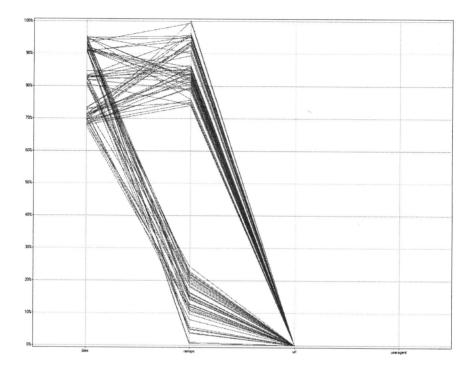

Figure 7.4. A plot of the "Code-red" worm access pattern

Even without knowing the contents of the web site, it is difficult to believe that there would be four sets of pages that would give rise to such access patterns. Indeed, the four patterns are quite distinct when compared to the rest of the subplots of the trellis plot. If we draw on knowledge about the contents of the website the game is immediately up.

There are one or two additional suspicious looking candidates, but viewing the request themselves gives that game away. It is not unreasonable to view the requests to eliminate suspects; we envision this method as mainly useful for the system administrator of the site, i.e. someone that is familiar with the site and and manner in which it is used. Indeed someone who was not familiar with the site could not make the sort of security policy decision on the spot that we alluded to in the introduction to the paper.

The four suspicious request patterns may be indicative of worm activity and merit further investigation. Dissecting the clusters with regards to the number of different requests results in:

Pattern 1 Six different requests.

Pattern 2 Ten different requests.

Pattern 3 One request.

Pattern 4 One request.

```
"GET /MSADC/root.exe?/c+dir HTTP/1.0"
"GET /_vti_bin/..%255c../..%255c../..%255c../winnt/system32/cmd.exe?/
     c+dir HTTP/1.0"
"GET /c/winnt/system32/cmd.exe?/c+dir HTTP/1.0"
"GET /d/winnt/system32/cmd.exe?/c+dir HTTP/1.0"
"GET /scripts/root.exe?/c+dir HTTP/1.0"
"GET /scripts/..%255c../winnt/system32/cmd.exe?/c+dir HTTP/1.0"
```

Figure 7.5. The six different requests made by pattern 1 from Figure 7.3

Viewing the access requests themselves (we have refrained from a detailed listing of all of them here to save space, but Figure 7.5 lists the six requests of the first pattern) and searching computer security sources we find evidence of two different instances of Nimda [CER01b] in patterns one and two. These two worms seems to have invaded the same types of systems, given the similarities in the IP-address ranges they originate from. Nimda is interesting in that it attacks web servers (Microsoft IIS) by either scanning for back doors left by other successful worms (Code red), or by so called *Unicode attacks*, where the URL is modified (certain characters escaped) to avoid subroutines in the web server that clean the request of certain "dangerous" characters e.g. characters that modify the search path to requested resource.

The third pattern consists of only one type of access. It was found equally quickly in the literature, since it consists of one very long access request, designed to overflow a buffer in IIS [CER01a]. The Code red worm does not probe for a wide variety of weaknesses in IIS, as Nimda does, relying solely on the one buffer overflow to gain entrance.

Comparing these two worms is illustrative in that we see a marked difference in the range of IP-addresses of infected systems. We presume that this is because Nimda can infect not only web servers, but also web clients (Microsoft Internet Explorer 5.0)—when the user visits a subverted web page, or be attached as an email virus. Thus home users, who presumably does not run web servers on their home computers frequently, are susceptible to infection by Nimda. Nimda then goes on to spread through all available means, including scanning nearby IP segments for vulnerable web servers and hence end up in our logs.

Code red, on the other hand, relies solely on web server infection, and hence will infect other IP address ranges that have not been reserved by Internet service providers who cater predominantly to the home users. Therefore we see such a marked difference in the access pattern.

Pattern four is the *pièce de résistance* of the investigation. At the time of investigation, neither the literature nor any of the major security information sources on the Internet listed this particular access request in conjunction with any known worm. They did list several similar access requests (as they are part of larger class of IIS vulnerabilities), and indeed had we only looked at the access requests themselves we might have missed that pattern four is different from the Nimda patterns since the request strings themselves look strikingly similar. The request in question is

```
"GET /scripts/..%255c%255c../winnt/system32/cmd.exe?/c+dir HTTP/0.9"
```

Compare the similarity with the last request made in Figure 7.5. The total number of accesses was small; only 71 access requests (about on the same order as for Code red, and an order of magnitude less than Nimda). Another odd characteristic was that they were not repeated from the same system twice (with one or two exceptions). We concluded that we were either dealing with a careful worm writer, or perhaps not even a worm at all, but rather the activities of so called *script kiddies*, who follow a pre-made recipe found somewhere on the Internet "underground". As far as we could tell this was a new type of worm, or a new type of intrusive activity. In preparing the earlier version of this Chapter, published as [Axe03], a very detailed search of the available information sources revealed that these access requests had in fact been spotted earlier and identified as being the product of the manual application of the "cracking tool" sfind.exe [Jel02]. This tool is employed by the *pubstro* movement [Bra], that break into web and file servers in order to build a network of computers with which to distribute "warez" (software distributed in violation of copyright). We were justified in our observation that the access requests were very similar to Nimda and may have been mistaken as such had we only looked at the access requests in isolation. Indeed many system administrators let this particular activity go unnoticed, mistaking it for an instance of Nimda [Jel02].

We subsequently realized that not all malicious activity present in Figure 7.3 had been reported. There exists a final pattern of malicious activity, **pattern five** in the figure, consisting of two access requests, which are:

```
"GET /scripts/..%c0%af../winnt/system32/cmd.exe?/c+dir+c:\ HTTP/1.1"
"GET /scripts/.%252e/.%252e/winnt/system32/cmd.exe?/c+dir+c:\ HTTP/1.1"
```

It is interesting in that it consists of a very small number of actual accesses— much smaller than for the other patterns. The first of these requests is interesting in that it is very similar to one of the worm requests, namely:

```
"GET /scripts/..%c0%af../winnt/system32/cmd.exe?/c+dir HTTP/1.0"
```

Looking closer at the pattern, we see that the two parallel coordinate plots are similar but not exactly identical, one line differs. Studying the log records associated with these requests we find that they originate from six different IP addresses and that five of them match perfectly, while in one instance only one of the requests is made. In all cases this is the only traffic we see from these hosts. Studying the available sources we learn that this pattern is also indicative of the sfind.exe tool mentioned in the previous paragraph, though run with another set of options than in the previous instance. It is interesting to note that an order of magnitude less accesses is made using these options than the (presumably) more straightforward options that result in pattern number four.

Even though there are a few more patterns in the rest of the data similar to pattern five, on closer inspection of the actual access requests they turn out to be benign. We are confident that we have (finally) found all the troublesome access requests.

6. Discussion

It is interesting to discuss the limitations of this method especially in light of the fact that the first report on this experiment went to print without the fifth pattern having been detected. A sticking point when doing visualization is that we can only aid the human operator in doing the detection. No matter how perfect this visual aid, the operator can still make mistakes. In the trellis plot in this case there is a visually distinct difference between patterns one through four and the benign patterns in that the benign patterns have a lot less traffic, and hence stand out much less than the malicious traffic. From this perspective it becomes possible to explain why the operator would mistake pattern five for a benign pattern as the operator subconsciously makes the distinction between the visually heavier intrusive patterns and the visually lighter benign patterns. As we have seen this conclusion breaks down in the face of pattern five, as even though it is visually similar to the benign patterns, it is still indicative of an attempted intrusion. So as a pure detection tool, i.e. as a visual tool that could help the operator differentiate between malicious and benign accesses, this approach may leave something to be desired in the case where we have much in the way of benign traffic. As a result, we are now less convinced that this method is suitable in that respect than when the work was first published. However, as a method to correlate access requests already found suspicious, e.g. by running a honey pot or applying any of the other approaches that have been presented in this book, the method presented here should still be effective in the manner demonstrated by our experiment.

Another question mark regarding the applicability of these results is the issue of scalability. The log file we investigated has only 59 unique requests, and as earlier pointed out; more realistic log files from larger installations can contain as much as 200 000 unique requests. The method of inspecting the requests directly, using a trellis plot, as we have done here is unfeasible when the number of unique requests is as large as 200 000. We conjecture that a data set of not much more than on the order of 100 unique requests could be investigated using the method developed here.

We see two ways of addressing this problem to enable this method to scale to larger data sets.

The first is to reduce the number of requests before applying the visualization. One method of doing so could be to apply some form of anomaly detection to the requests, sorting out unusual requests, and then visualizing the output from the anomaly detection system to.[5] This would allow us to tell apart the malicious accesses from the inevitable false alarms that would creep into the output from the anomaly detection system. An advantage of such an approach is that it would allow the anomaly detection system to be tuned so that the number of false alarms were relatively high—and hence the likelihood of detection would be correspondingly higher—since we would not observe the output directly, but use it as input for our visualization method.

The other approach (perhaps most realistically used in conjunction with the first) is to reduce the number of unique requests by doing stepwise elimination, by first identifying two or more similar patterns and then combining them into one pattern (sub plot). Hereby iteratively reducing the number of subplots until it is small enough that an overview of all of them can be made, analogous with what we have performed in this experiment.

7. Conclusion

We have demonstrated that worm activity can be detected and analyzed by applying a trellis plot of parallel coordinate visualizations on the log of a small web server. The different requests made by worms can be correlated to the particular type of worm making the requests. Furthermore, the clusters formed by worm requests are markedly different from the clusters formed by benign requests *for the data set in this paper*. Other patterns of malicious requests were also found, one which was *worm like* and distinct from benign access requests and one that was not, and as a result was overlooked when the first version of this paper was published. The visualization was successful even though the number of data points visualized was larger than what is generally considered the limit for such methods.

Four different worm (or worm like) activities were found. Two of these were found to be indicative of the Nimda worm, one of the Code red worm, and the last two of a then largely unknown malicious activity, later identified as emanating from the manual application of the tool `sfind.exe`.

8. Future Work

This investigation has really only scratched the surface of both what security relevant information is hiding in data sets such as this and of what visualization

---

[5]i.e. the approach taken in Chapter 4.

in general, and how parallel coordinate plots in particular can be brought to bear to extract it. Also, the data set itself could be expanded with more realistic traffic, and more advanced simulated attacks.

Chapter 8

EPILOGUE

1. Results in Perspective

Computer security must rely – in a broad sense – on *perimeter* defenses. The term *perimeter* should not be interpreted too literally here; it need not have a literal interpretation as in case of firewalls etc. To our mind, other approaches that serve to separate the protected entity from the attacker's sphere of observation and influence also falls under this heading, such as the approach of statically (or dynamically) verify that source code is free of security defects etc. cf. the concept of *prevention* in Halme et. al. [HB95], described in Chapter 2.

Perimeter defenses should be employed in depth. That is, just because one has been granted—or otherwise gained—access through the outer perimeter, one should not have free reign of the system.

However, no matter how well protected a system is, there will always be chinks in its armor, and thus some sort of surveillance and response system must be in place to detect and deal with intruders as and when they appear. This system can sometimes possess a high degree of autonomy as is the case with virus scanners, spam filters (using signatures of known spam) and signature based intrusion detection systems. We would argue that in the general case, dealing with the more imaginative threats, a human operator needs to be in the loop and in order to be effective there should be tool support that enables her to quickly gain an understanding of the situation. We call this the principle of *surveillance* to set it apart from more traditional intrusion detection system principles. To believe that automated systems could deal with other than the most routine threats is overly optimistic, as the attacker in many cases could analyze the defenses for weaknesses and attack us there, to wit: "there's no equipment that man's ingenuity can devise that man's ingenuity can't also defeat" [KCBH96, p. 51]. No perimeter defense, however strong, will not last if it is left unguarded, providing the attacker with ample time to analyze and ultimately defeat it.

2.   Further Reading

The first mention in the literature of the idea to apply visualization to the field of computer security (specifically, intrusion detection) of which we are aware of is by Vert et al. in [VFM98].[1] At the time of writing the area has seen more investigation, and as such we will limit the treatment here to selected applications of visualization in an intrusion detection setting much as ours, where the intent has been to apply scientific visualization to help the operator gain insight into the security state of the monitored systems.

The work of Vert. et al presents a preliminary visualization of the security state of a computer system, by way of a spherical geometric primitive called a *Spicule*—the characteristics of which are investigated—but provides no opinion on how that security state should be calculated. More recently Erbacher et. al. [EWF02] has presented work building on the previous work by Frincke et. al. [FTM98]. This work is based on encoding information about network traffic and alarms from a network of intrusion detection sensors, as glyphs onto a stylized map of the network.

A small subfield (e.g. [ROT03, JWK02, LZHM02]) of anomaly detection and visualization has arisen through the application of self-organizing maps (also called Kohonen maps) [Koh01] to intrusion detection. The question of visualization arises because the Kohonen map itself is a visual representation of an underlying neural network model. The work cited above shares the characteristic that they all build some neural network model of network traffic or host data and then present the resulting two dimensional scatter plot to the user. The scatter plot typically illustrates various clusters within the data. A problem here is that the interpretation of the plot is known to be quite tricky [Koh01].

Girardin et al. [GB98, Gir99] also uses self-organizing maps, but stresses the link to the human operator. They also utilize other visualization methods in addition to the self-organizing map itself, using the self-organizing map as an automatic clustering mechanism. They report on successful experiments on data with known intrusions. For input data they use connection statistics etc. from TCP/IP traffic as their input data. While they study parameters of TCP/IP connections, they do not study the data transferred.

Theo et al. [TMWZ02] visualize communication between pairs of routers on the Internet using the BGP (Border Gateway Protocol) routing protocol. Their choice of problem and visualization techniques are different from the one presented here, and they do not delve as deeply into the analysis of the

---

[1]Predating this, the idea of applying visualization to intrusion detection was suggested to us by Professor Erland Jonsson at a meeting in the autumn of 1996.

security problems they detect (they are not as clearly *security problems*), but they do visualize a greater amount of data more compactly than done in this book and still manage to detect anomalies in the BGP traffic. This work has later been continued by adding a *NIDES* [AFV95] based anomaly based intrusion detection component and visualizing the output of the classifier together with the BGP update messages. Another view then lets the user do *what if* calculations setting different classifier parameters with visual feedback [TZT+04].

In a similar vein, visualizing network flows (i.e. records that contain abstract information about communication sessions between computers such as source and destination IP addresses, how many bytes were transferred etc.) has been studied recently by Yin et al. [YYT+04]. Here parallel coordinate visualization is used (as we do) to selected parameters of these *netflow* records to detect anomalies in network traffic.

A quick survey of the available commercial intrusion detection systems was also made. Only two systems uses any degree of visualization in our sense of the word. The first is *CA Network Forensics*[2] which uses N-gram clustering followed by a three dimensional visual display of the clusters. On the surface the visual representation of the data in the clusters is similar to the one presented in Chapter 4 (i.e. a general 3D network) but while the graphs may look similar they express very different relations. There is no discussion as to the interpretation of these graphs and the underlying structure of the data is not allowed to influence the visualization.

The second is *Lancope Therminator*[3] which is based on the Therminator project described in [ZME04]. Therminator is a network level anomaly detection tool inspired by methods from the field of statistical physics. The anomaly detector works by building a model of network traffic as a modified *Ehrenfest urn model*, the parameters of which are (in addition to other processing) visualized as three dimensional bar charts, to give the user an overview of the state space of the model. The authors report on experiments where anomalies have been injected into the traffic with the corresponding diagrams clearly showing a marked difference between the anomalous event and the steady state. The authors do not emphasize the visualization portion of the work presented in [ZME04] and it is difficult to ascertain the degree to which the visualization helps the operator gain insight into exactly what caused the deviation from the normal graph, even though it seems promising.

The literature in the area has recently grown to become quite extensive, and we cannot do it justice here. The interested reader is referred to [BCLY04] as a starting point.

---

[2]"http://www3.ca.com/Solutions/Product.asp?ID=4856". Verified 2004-12-20.
[3]"http://www.lancope.com". Verified 2004-12-20.

3.   Conclusions and Future Work

The marriage between visualization and intrusion detection seems at the outset a happy one. The application of visualization seems to bring benefits in the form of increased understanding of the security state of the monitored systems.

Even though the usability of intrusion detection systems and the application of the principle of surveillance to the problem has seen some interest in recent years, much work remains to be done. The current research (including this monograph) really only scratches the surface of the possibilities in the field. Even though early results seem very promising there still remains much research to be done by including the actual operator. Notably absent from current research are *user studies*. These are more difficult to conduct than one might first imagine. The process of classifying behavior into malicious and benign, using approaches such as ours, is a highly skilled task (where operator training would probably have a major influence on the results). It is also a highly cognitive task, and hence difficult to observe objectively. If such studies are to be of value they would almost certainly be costly, and the state of research into how to measure and interpret the results may not be sufficiently well developed to justify such experiments. .

If the authors were to single out one area presented in this book as the most promising for further research it would be the application of visualization to make machine learning systems more accessible to the user. We have not found much in the literature in the way of applying visualization to this area, and based on the early results in this book the area looks promising.

References

[AFV95]   D Anderson, T Frivold, and A Valdes. Next-generation intrusion-detection expert system (NIDES). Technical Report SRI-CSL-95-07, Computer Science Laboratory, SRI International, Menlo Park, CA 94025-3493, USA, May 1995. {**51, 131**}

[ALGJ98]   Stefan Axelsson, Ulf Lindqvist, Ulf Gustafson, and Erland Jonsson. An approach to UNIX security logging. In *Proceedings of the 21st National Information Systems Security Conference*, pages 62–75, Crystal City, Arlington, VA, USA, 5–8 October 1998. NIST, National Institute of Standards and Technology/National Computer Security Center. {**21, 26, 27, 35**}

[And80]   James P. Anderson. Computer security threat monitoring and surveillance. Technical Report Contract 79F26400, James P. Anderson Co., Box 42, Fort Washington, PA, 19034, USA, 26 February revised 15 April 1980. {**20, 25**}

[Axe00a]   Stefan Axelsson. The base-rate fallacy and the difficulty of intrusion detection. *ACM Transactions on Information and System Security (TISSEC)*, 3(3):186–205, 2000. {**31, 59**}

[Axe00b]   Stefan Axelsson. A preliminary attempt to apply detection and estimation theory to intrusion detection. Technical Report 00–4, Department of Computer Engineering, Chalmers University of Technology, SE–412 96, Göteborg, Sweden, March 2000. {**22**}

[Axe03]   Stefan Axelsson. Visualization for intrusion detection: Hooking the worm. In *The proceedings of the 8th European Symposium on Research in Computer Security (ESORICS 2003)*, volume 2808 of *LNCS*, Gjøvik, Norway, 13–15 October 2003. Springer Verlag. {**13, 111, 124**}

[Axe04a]   Stefan Axelsson. Combining a bayesian classifier with visualisation: Understanding the IDS. In Carla Brodley, Philip Chan, Richard Lippman, and Bill Yurcik, editors, *Proceedings of the 2004 ACM workshop on Visualization and data mining for computer security*, pages 99–108, Washington DC, USA, 29 October 2004. ACM Press. Held in conjunction with the Eleventh ACM Conference on Computer and Communications Security. {**69**}

134

[Axe04b]   Stefan Axelsson. Visualising intrusions: Watching the webserver. In *Proceedings of the 19th IFIP International Information Security Conference (SEC2004)*, Tolouse, France, 22–27 August 2004. IFIP. {**49**}

[BAJ03]   Emilie Lundin Barse, Magnus Almgren, and Erland Jonsson. Consolidation and evaluation of ids taxonomies. In *Proceedings of the eighth Nordic Workshop on Secure IT systems (NordSec 2003)*, Gjøvik, Norway, October 2003. {**28, 29**}

[Bar04a]   Emilie Lundin Barse. Extracting attack manifestations to determine log data requirements for intrusion detection. Technical Report 04-01, Department of Computer Engineering, Chalmers University of Technology, Göteborg, Sweden, June 2004. {**26**}

[Bar04b]   Emilie Lundin Barse. *Logging for intrusion and fraud detection*. PhD thesis, School of Computer Science and Engineering, Chalmers University of Technology, Göteborg, Sweden, 2004. {**27**}

[BCLY04]   Carla Brodley, Philip Chan, Richard Lippman, and Bill Yurcik, editors. *VizSEC/DMSEC '04: Proceedings of the 2004 ACM workshop on Visualization and data mining for computer security*, Washington DC, USA, 2004. ACM Press. {**131**}

[BKS01]   Barry Becker, Ron Kohavi, and Dan Sommerfield. Visualizing the simple Bayesian classifier. In Usama Fayyad, Georges Grinstein, and Andreas Wierse, editors, *Information Visualization in Data Mining and Knowledge Discovery*, chapter 18, pages 237–249. Morgan Kaufmann Publishers, San Francisco, 2001. {**107**}

[Bra]   Richard Braithwaite. The 'pubstro' Phenomenon: Robin Hoods of the Internet. Avaliable as: "http://www.deakin.edu.au/infosys/docs/seminars/-handouts/RichardBraithwaite.pdf" Verified: 2003–07–24. {**124**}

[CEC91]   Commission of the European Communities. *Information Technology Security Evaluation Criteria*, June 1991. Version 1.2. {**2**}

[CER01a]   CERT Advisory CA-2001-19 'Code Red' Worm Exploiting Buffer Overflow in IIS Indexing Service DLL. CERT Advisory by CERT/CC, Email: cert@cert.org, CERT Coordination Center, Software Engineering Institute, Carnegie Mellon University, Pittsburgh PA 15213-3890, U.S.A., 19 July revised 17 January 2001. "http://www.cert.org". {**50, 111, 123**}

[CER01b]   CERT Advisory CA-2001-26 Nimda Worm. CERT advisory by CERT/CC, Email: cert@cert.org, CERT Coordination Center, Software Engineering Institute, Carnegie Mellon University, Pittsburgh PA 15213-3890, U.S.A., 18 September revised 25 September 2001. "http://www.cert.org". {**50, 112, 123**}

[CMS99]   Stuart K. Card, Jock D. MacKinlay, and Ben Shneiderman. *Readings in Information Visualization—Using Vision to Think*. Series in Interactive Technologies. Morgan Kaufmann, Morgan Kaufmann Publishers, 340 Pine Street, Sixth Floor, San Fransisco, CA 94104-3205, USA, first edition, 1999. ISBN 1-55860-533-9. {**4, 5, 49, 92**}

[DBS92]   Herve Debar, Monique Becker, and Didier Siboni. A neural network component for an intrusion detection system. In *Proceedings of the 1992 IEEE Computer*

Sociecty Symposium on Research in Security and Privacy, pages 240–250, Oakland, CA, USA, May 1992. IEEE, IEEE Computer Society Press, Los Alamitos, CA, USA. {**44**}

[Dea72]   B. H. Deatherage. Auditory and other sensory forms of information. In HP Van Cott and RG Kinkade, editors, *Human Engineering Guide to Equipment design*. Army, Navy, Air Force, 1972. {**37**}

[EWF02]   Robert F. Erbacher, Kenneth L. Walker, and Deborah A. Frincke. Intrusion and Misuse Detection in Large-Scale Systems. *Computer Graphics and Applications*, 22(1):38–48, January 2002. {**130**}

[FGM⁺99]   R. Fielding, J. Gettys, J. Mogul, H. Frystyk, L. Masinter, P. Leach, and T. Berners-Lee. RFC 2616—Hypertext Transfer Protocol—HTTP/1.1. Request for Comment 2616, The Internet Society, 1999. {**72, 98**}

[Fra94]   Jeremy Frank. Artificial intelligence and intrusion detection: Current and future directions. Division of Computer Science, University of California at Davis, Davis, CA. 95619, 9 June 1994. {**21**}

[FSBK03]   Laura Feinstein, Dan Schnackenberg, Ravindra Balupari, and Darrell Kindred. Statistical Approaches to DDoS Attack Detection and Response. In *Proceedings of the DARPA Information Survivability Conference and Exposition*, page 303. IEEE Computer Society, IEEE, 22–24 April 2003. {**119**}

[FTM98]   Deborah A. Frincke, Donald L. Tobin, and Jesse C. McConnell. Research Issues in Cooperative Intrusion Detection Between Multiple Domains. In *Proceedings of Recent advances in intrusion detetection RAID'98*, 1998. {**130**}

[GB98]   Luc Girardin and Dominique Brodbeck. A visual approach for monitoring logs. In *The Proceedings of the 12th Systems Administration Conference (LISA '98)*, pages 299–308, Boston, Massachusetts, USA, 6–11 December 1998. The USENIX Association. {**130**}

[Gir99]   Luc Girardin. An eye on network intruder-administrator shootouts. In *The Proceedings of the Workshop on Intrusion Detection and Network Monitoring*, Santa Clara, California, USA, 9–12 April 1999. The USENIX Association. {**130**}

[GLC⁺98]   Isaac Graf, Richard Lippman, Robert Cunningham, David Fried, Kris Kendall, Seth Webster, and Marc Zissman. Results of DARPA 1998 offline intrusion detection evaluation. "http://www.ll.mit.edu/IST/ideval", December 15 1998. {**42, 46**}

[Gol00]   Dieter Gollmann. On the verification of cryptographic protocols. Presentation at Karlstad University, 11 February 2000. {**17**}

[Gra02]   Paul Graham. A plan for spam. http://www.paulgraham.com/spam.html, August 2002. {**9, 70**}

[HB95]   Lawrence R. Halme and Kenneth R. Bauer. AINT misbehaving—A taxonomy of anti-intrusion techniques. In *Proceedings of the 18th National Information Systems Security Conference*, pages 163–172, Baltimore, MD, USA, October 1995. NIST, National Institute of Standards and Technology/National Computer Security Center. {**15, 129**}

136

[HL93]   Paul Helman and Gunar Liepins. Statistical foundations of audit trail analysis for the detection of computer misuse. *IEEE Transactions on Software Engineering*, 19(9):886–901, September 1993. {**27, 42, 44, 45**}

[HLF⁺01]   Joshua W. Haines, Richard P. Lippmann, David J. Fried, Eushiuan Tran, Steve Boswell, and Marc A. Zissman. 1999 DARPA intrusion detection system evaluation: Design and procedures. Technical Report ESC-TR-99-061, MIT Lincoln Laboratory Technical Report, February 2001. {**43**}

[Ins97]   Alfred Inselberg. Multidimensional Detective. In *Proceedings of InfoVis'97, IEEE Symposium on Information Visualization*, pages 100–107. IEEE Information visualisation, IEEE, 1997. {**13, 114, 115**}

[Jel02]   Peter Jelver. Pubstro-hacking—Systematic Establishment of Warez Servers on Windows Internet Servers. Avaliable as: "http://www.esec.dk/pubstro.pdf" Verified: 2003–07–24, 23 July 2002. {**124**}

[Jon98]   Erland Jonsson. An integrated framework for security and dependability. In *Proceedings of the New Security Paradigms Workshop 1998*, Charlottesville, VA, USA, 22–25 September 1998. {**2**}

[JWK02]   Chaivat Jirapummin, Naruemon Wattanapongsakorn, and Prasert Kanthamanon. Hybrid neural networks for intrusion detection system. In *Proceedings of The 2002 International Technical Conference on Circuits/Systems, Computers and Communications (ITC-CSCC 2002)*, pages 928–931, Phuket, Thailand, 16–19 July 2002. {**130**}

[KCBH96]   Andrew Kain, Ken Connor, Paul Brown, and Neil Hanson. *SAS Security Handbook*. William Heinemann, Reed Intl. Books Ltd., Michelin House, 81 Fulhamn Rd., London SW3 6RB, first edition, 1996. ISBN 0-434-00306-9. {**129**}

[KMRV03]   Christopher Kruegel, Darren Mutz, William Robertson, and Fredrik Valleur. Bayesian event classification for intrusion detection. In *Proceedings of the 19th Annual Computer Security Applications Conference*, Las Vegas, Nevada, USA, December 2003. {**44, 45**}

[KMT04]   Kevin S. Killourhy, Roy A. Maxion, and Kymie M. C. Tan. A defence-centric taxonomy based on attack manifestations. In *Proceedings of the International Conference on Dependable Systems and Networks (DSN 2004)*, Florence, Italy, June 2004. {**26**}

[Koh01]   Teuvo Kohonen. *Self-Organizing Maps*, volume 30 of *Springer Series in Information Sciences*. Springer Verlag, Third edition, 2001. ISBN 3-540-67921-9, ISSN 0720-678X. {**130**}

[KSD96]   Ron Kohavi, Dan Sommerfield, and James Dougherty. Data mining using MLC++: A machine learning library in C++. In *Tools with Artificial Intelligence*, pages 234–245. IEEE Computer Society Press, 1996. {**107**}

[KV03]   C. Kruegel and G. Vigna. Anomaly detection of web-based attacks. In *Proceedings of the 10th ACM Conference on Computer and Communication Security (CCS '03)*, pages 251–261, Washington DC, USA, October 2003. ACM Press. {**67**}

[LB98]   Terran Lane and Carla E. Brodie. Temporal sequence learning and data reduction for anomaly detection. In *5th ACM Conference on Computer & Communications Security*, pages 150–158, San Francisco, California, USA, 3–5 November 1998. {**27, 41**}

[LBMC94]   Carl E Landwehr, Alan R Bull, John P McDermott, and William S Choi. A taxonomy of computer program security flaws. *ACM Computing Surveys*, 26(3):211–254, September 1994. {**25, 26**}

[Lee99]   Wenke Lee. A data mining framework for building intrusion detection models. In *IEEE Symposium on Security and Privacy*, pages 120–132, Berkeley, California, May 1999. {**29, 44, 45**}

[LFG$^+$00]   Richard P. Lippmann, David J. Fried, Isaac Graf, Joshua W. Haines, Kristoper R. Kendall, David McClung, Dan Weber, Seth E. Webster, Dan Wyschogrod, Robert K. Cunningham, and Marc A. Zissman. Evaluating intrusion detection systems: the 1998 DARPA off-line intrusion detection evaluation. In *Proceedings of the 2000 DARPA Information Survivability Conference and Exposition*, volume 2, 2000. {**43**}

[LFM$^+$02]   Wenke Lee, Wei Fan, Matt Miller, Sal Stolfo, and Erez Zadok. Towards cost-sensitive modeling for intrusion detection. *Journal of Computer Security*, 10(1), 2002. {**46**}

[LGG$^+$98]   Richard P. Lippmann, Isaac Graf, S. L. Garfinkel, A. S. Gorton, K. R. Kendall, D. J. McClung, D. J. Weber, S. E. Webster, D. Wyschogrod, and M. A. Zissman. The 1998 DARPA/AFRL off-line intrusion detection evaluation. The First Workshop on Recent Advances in Intrusion Detection (RAID-98), Lovain-la-Neuve, Belgium, 14–16 September 1998. {**42, 71**}

[LJ97]   Ulf Lindqvist and Erland Jonsson. How to systematically classify computer security intrusions. In *Proceedings of the 1997 IEEE Symposium on Security & Privacy*, pages 154–163, Oakland, CA, USA, 4–7 May 1997. IEEE, IEEE Computer Society Press, Los Alamitos, CA, USA. {**25, 26**}

[LMPT98]   Ulf Lindqvist, Douglas Moran, Phillip A Porras, and Mabry Tyson. Designing IDLE: The intrusion data library enterprise. Abstract presented at RAID '98 (First International Workshop on the Recent Advances in Intrusion Detection), Louvain-la-Neuve, Belgium, 14–16 September 1998. {**22**}

[LMS00]   W. Lee, M. Miller, and S. Stolfo. Toward cost-sensitive modeling for intrusion detection, 2000. {**22**}

[LX01]   Wenke Lee and Dong Xiang. Information-theoretic measures for anomaly detection. In *IEEE Symposium on Security and Privacy*, Oakland, California, USA, 14–16 May 2001. IEEE. {**63**}

[LZHM02]   P. Lichodzijewski, A.N. Zincir-Heywood, and Heywood M.I. Host-based intrusion detection using self-organizing maps. In *The proceedings of the IEEE International Joint Conference on Neural Networks*. IEEE, May 2002. {**130**}

[Mat96]   Robert Matthews. Base-rate errors and rain forecasts. *Nature*, 382(6594):766, 29 August 1996. {**32**}

[Mat97]   Robert Matthews. Decision-theoretic limits on earthquake prediction. *Geophys. J. Int.*, 131(3):526–529, December 1997. {**32**}

[Max03]   Roy A. Maxion. Masquerade detection using enriched command lines. In *International Conference on Dependable Systems & Networks (DSN-03)*, pages 5–14, San Fransisco, California, USA, 22–25 June 2003. IEEE. {**26**}

[MC03]   Matthew V. Mahoney and Philip K. Chan. An analysis of the 1999 DARPA/Lincoln Laboratory evaluation data for network anomaly detection. In Giovanni Vigna, Chrisopher Kruegel, and Erland Jonsson, editors, *Recent Advances in Intrusion Detection: 6th International Symposium RAID 2003*, LNCS, pages 220–237. Springer Verlag GmbH, November 2003. ISBN: 3-540-40878-9. {**42, 73**}

[McH00]   John McHugh. Testing intrusion detection systems: a critique of the 1998 and 1999 darpa intrusion detection system evaluations as performed by lincoln laboratory. *ACM Trans. Inf. Syst. Secur.*, 3(4):262–294, 2000. {**43, 50, 71**}

[Mea93]   Catherine A Meadows. An outline of a taxonomy of computer security research and development. In *Proceedings of the 1992–1993 ACM SIGSAC New Security Paradigms Workshop*, pages 33–35, Little Compton, Rhode Island, 22–24 September 1992 and 3–5 August 1993. IEEE Computer Society Press. {**2**}

[MW04]   T.A. Meyer and B. Whateley. SpamBayes: Effective open-source, Bayesian based, email classification system. In *Proceedings of the First Conference on Email and Anti-Spam (CEAS)*, Mountain View, CA, USA, 30–31 July 2004. {**11, 90, 91**}

[NP89]   Peter G Neumann and Donn B Parker. A summary of computer misuse techniques. In *Proceedings of the 12th National Computer Security Conference*, pages 396–407, Baltimore, Maryland, 10–13 October 1989. {**26**}

[Nyg94]   Else Nygren. Moderna tider: teknikutveckling inom medicinsk service. Technical report, Vårdförbundet SHSTF 42, Stockholm, Sweden, 1994. ISBN91-7043-021-7, ISSN 0349-1757, In Swedish. {**37**}

[Pfl97]   Charles P. Pfleeger. *Security in Computing*. Prentice Hall, second edition, 1997. ISBN 0-13-185794-0. {**111**}

[Pie48]   G. McGuire Pierce. Destruction by demolition, incendiaries and sabotage. Field training manual, Fleet Marine Force, US Marine Corps, 1943–1948. Reprinted: Paladin Press, PO 1307, Boulder CO, USA. {**3, 32**}

[PN98]   Thomas H. Ptacek and Timothy N. Newsham. Insertion, evasion, and denial of service: Eluding network intrusion detection. Technical report, Secure Networks Inc., January 1998. {**27**}

[Pro03]   Niels Provos. Improving host security with system call policies. In *Proceedings of the 12th USENIX Security Symposium*, Washington D.C., USA, August 2003. {**69**}

[Ras86]   Jens Rasmussen. *Information processing and human-machine interaction, An appoach to cognitive engineering*. Elsevier Science Publishing Co., Inc., 52 Vanderbild Avenue, New York, New York 10017, first edition, 1986. {**36**}

[RDL87]   Jens Rasmussen, Keith Duncan, and Jacques Leplat, editors. *New Technology and Human Error (New Technologies and Work)*. John Wiley & Sons, March 1987. {**6, 7, 73**}

[RN95]   Stuart J. Russel and Peter Norvig. *Artificial Intelligence—A Modern Approach*, chapter 14, pages 426–435. Prentice Hall Series in Artificial Intelligence. Prentice Hall International, Inc., London, UK, first edition, 1995. Exercise 14.3. {**33**}

[Roe99]   Martin Roesch. Snort: Lightweight intrusion detection for networks. In *Proceedings of the 13th USENIX conference on System administration*, pages 229–238. USENIX Association, 1999. {**63**}

[ROT03]   Manikantan Ramadas, Shawn Ostermann, and Brett Tjaden. Detecting anomalous network traffic with self-organizing maps. In *Proceedings of the Sixth International Symposium on Recent Advances in Intrusion Detection*, LNCS, Pittsburgh, PA, USA, 8–10 September 2003. Springer Verlag. {**130**}

[Spe01]   Robert Spence. *Information Visualization*. ACM Press Books, Pearson education ltd., Edinburgh Gate, Harlow, Essex CM20 2JE, England, first edition, 2001. ISBN 0-201-59626-1. {**4, 49, 114, 118**}

[Sto95]   Clifford Stoll. *The Cuckoo's Egg: Tracking a Spy Through the Maze of Computer Espionage*. Pocket Books, July 1995. {**36**}

[TM02]   Kymie M. C. Tan and Roy A. Maxion. "Why 6?" Defining the operational limits of stide, an anomaly-based intrusion detector. In *Proceedings of the 2002 IEEE Symposium on Security and Privacy*. IEEE Computer Society, 2002. {**91**}

[TMWZ02]   Soon Tee Teoh, Kwan-Liu Ma, S. Felix Wu, and Xiaoliang Zhao. Case Study: Interactive Visualization for Internet Security. In *Proceedings of IEEE Visualization 2002*, The Boston Park Plaza hotel, Boston, Massachusetts, USA, 27 October to 1 November 2002. IEEE Computer society. {**130**}

[Tre68]   Harry L. Van Trees. *Detection, Estimation, and Modulation Theory, Part I, Detection, Estimation, and Linear Modulation Theory*. John Wiley and Sons, Inc., 1968. {**23, 24, 29, 41, 42**}

[Tuf01]   Edward R. Tufte. *The Visual Display of Quantitative Information*. Graphics Press, second edition, May 2001. ISBN 0–96–139214–2. {**74, 75, 93**}

[TZT+04]   Soon Tee Teoh, Ke Zhang, Shih-Ming Tseng, Kwan-Liu Ma, and S. Felix Wu. Combining visual and automated data mining for near-real-time anomaly detection and analysis in bgp. In *VizSEC/DMSEC '04: Proceedings of the 2004 ACM workshop on Visualization and data mining for computer security*, pages 35–44, Washington DC, USA, 2004. ACM Press. {**131**}

[USA01]   'Ny Times' Outage Caused by Nimda virus. "http://www.usatoday.com/tech/-news/2001/11/01/new-york-times-outage.htm", 1 December 2001. Verified 2003–04–11. {**112**}

[VFM98]   Greg Vert, Deborah A. Frincke, and Jesse C. McConnell. A Visual Mathematical Model for Intrusion Detection. In *Proceedings of the 21st National Information*

Systems Security Conference, Crystal City, Arlington, VA, USA, 5–8 October 1998. NIST, National Institute of Standards and Technology/National Computer Security Center. {**130**}

[VL89]   H S Vaccaro and G E Liepins. Detection of anomalous computer session activity. In *Proceedings of the 1989 IEEE Symposium on Security and Privacy*, pages 280–289, Oakland, California, 1–3 May 1989. {**44**}

[VRB04]   G. Vigna, W. Robertson, and D. Balzarotti. Testing Network-based Intrusion Detection Signatures Using Mutant Exploits. In *Proceedings of the ACM Conference on Computer and Communication Security (ACM CCS)*, Washington, DC, October 2004. {**43**}

[VS00]   Alfonso Valdes and Keith Skinner. Adaptive, model-based monitoring for cyber attack detection. In H. Debar, L. Me, and F. Wu, editors, *Recent Advances in Intrusion Detection (RAID 2000)*, volume 1907 of *Lecture Notes in Computer Science*, pages 80–92, Toulouse, France, October 2000. Springer-Verlag, Berlin—Heidelberg, Germany. {**70**}

[WFP99]   Christina Warrender, Stephanie Forrest, and Barak Perlmutter. Detecting intrusions using system calls: Alternative data models. In *IEEE Symposium on Security and Privacy*, pages 133–145, Berkeley, California, May 1999. {**42, 44, 45, 91, 98, 99**}

[WH99]   Christopher D. Wickens and Justin G. Hollands. *Engineering Psychology and Human Performance*. Prentice Hall, third edition, September 1999. ISBN 0–32–104711–7. {**6, 7, 73, 89**}

[Wic92]   Christopher Wickens. *Engineering psychology and human performance*. Harper-Collins Publishers Inc., 10 East 53rd Street, New York, NY 10022, second edition, 1992. {**36, 37**}

[Yer04]   William S. Yerazunis. The spam-filtering accuracy plateau at 99.9% accuracy and how to get past it. In *Proceedings of the 2004 MIT Spam Conference*, MIT Cambridge Massachusetts, USA, 16 January 2004. Revised 6 February. {**11, 82, 90, 91**}

[YYT⁺04]   Xiaoxin Yin, William Yurcik, Michael Treaster, Yifan Li, and Kiran Lakkaraju. Visflowconnect: netflow visualizations of link relationships for security situational awareness. In *VizSEC/DMSEC '04: Proceedings of the 2004 ACM workshop on Visualization and data mining for computer security*, pages 26–34, Washington DC, USA, 2004. ACM Press. {**131**}

[ZME04]   John Zachary, John McEachen, and Dan Ettlich. Conversation exchange dynamics for real-time network monitoring and anomaly detection. In *IWIA '04: Proceedings of the Second IEEE International Information Assurance Workshop (IWIA'04)*, page 59. IEEE Computer Society, 2004. {**131**}

Author Index

142

Index